This book is dedicated to my five

Amanda, Wendy, Jill, Tess and Rita.

I could not be more proud of their accomplishments and the way they have turned out. They know that anything worth anything takes time and hard work. They are my best friends and the lights of my life.

I especially want to thank my wife, Jennifer, who has encouraged me over the years especially during some trying times dealing with the difficult parts of a business cycle.

I want to thank my mom and dad for raising me to think for myself.

Finally, this book is for Frank and Sam, the greatest grandfathers any kid could ever have...I miss you both.

Copyright ©2012 Craig Wieland, All rights reserved.
Unauthorized duplication is prohibited.
Printed in the United States of America

Craig Wieland Publishing
4162 English Oak
Lansing, Michigan 48911
cw@craigwieland.com
1-(517)-908 0591

ISBN 978-0-9882294-0-2

1

Forward

<u>Why</u> do conservatives believe <u>what</u> they believe?

In this book, you will discover the answer.

Conservatives don't like nuances. We have a hard time seeing both sides of an issue and then coming down squarely in the middle. No, conservatives believe that there are some positions that are right, and others that are wrong. However, we do understand that when we articulate our deeply-held positions, we must do so in a spirit of humility and grace. Never from a condescending position or a "righteous" attitude, but in deference to the other side, trying hard to show why we believe we are right, and hoping our argument is convincing enough to convert the skeptic.

Conservatism is best described using specific subjects, rather than principles, since both liberals and conservatives claim many of the same principles as their own. For instance, both believe in personal responsibility, honesty, hard work, compassion, civility, and dozens of other fine attributes as guiding principles that define their thinking, but both sides have very different beliefs regarding Israel, abortion, marriage, subsidies, tax policy, entitlements, environmental policy and government mandates.

In this book, I provide the conservative belief on sixty-one subjects, including the reason why we believe this way. In my previous book, *Pointed Poems*, I chose thirty subjects and did the same, although using a different format that contained rhymes and cartoon illustrations. It was due to the success of this first book that I felt the need to expand on what it means to be a conservative and why. It is my hope that if you are already a conservative, you will appreciate the provocative, straightforward way that I address our highly-valued beliefs. If you are not a conservative, I hope you will consider our positions and even if you don't end up agreeing with us, you will know the "why" behind our strong convictions on so many important issues.

Over the past couple years, I have asked hundreds of people to do something for me. I have asked them to picture, in their mind's eye, a train crash. After they told me they had the image, I asked them a second question: "*Did you picture the train crashing from a safe distance away, or did you picture yourself on the train as it crashed*?" Without exception, everyone always pictured themselves a safe distance away. Unfortunately, this is a metaphor for our country. Given the track we are on as a nation, there is going to be a crash. However, instead of dealing with this situation as if we were personally going to be harmed, we deal with it abstractly, almost as if we were a witness standing a safe distance away. I'm sorry, my friend, but you and I are on the train. I, for one, would like to see us avoid the crash, and thinking and acting conservatively will accomplish this task.

Why Me?

Why do I get to decide what conservatives believe and their reasoning? Even though I have been a conservative my whole life, more importantly, I have taken the time to develop my views in a structured, systematic, and unemotional manner. Finally, I have subjected my conclusions to many recognized conservative leaders throughout the country and have met with their approval. Here is a sampling of what they said about my first book, *Pointed Poems, Tools for Teaching Conservative Thinking...*

"Craig Wieland has combined two disciplines — poetry and art — into a highly visual and wonderfully readable series of editorials that will delight the eye and inspire the mind. "
-Cal Thomas
Syndicated Columnist

"Craig Wieland has pulled off a miracle with his clever Pointed Poems, *bringing levity and humor to the otherwise painful negativity of the liberal derangement syndrome. A good belly laugh will help us keep fighting the liberal curse."*
-Ted Nugent
Musician and Activist

"Teaching your kids conservative values is incredibly important. Craig's book does so in a way that is both fun and serious at the same time. Your kids will enjoy reading the poems and as a parent you will be confident that they are learning the values that you hold dear."
Ralph Reed
Chairman, Faith and Freedom Coalition

"As conservatives, we know how important it is to teach our values to our kids and grandkids. Craig's book offers excellent insights to accomplishing this critical task."
-Dan Quayle
Vice President

"Pointed Poems *clearly shows how to help kids "get the point" about responsible citizenship."*
-John Ashcroft
US. Senator and United States Attorney General

"Craig is a sharp-eyed, innovative, thought-provoking writer for the conservative cause."
-Tim Phillips
Americans for Prosperity

"*Craig's book should be given by conservatives to every young person they know.*"
-Frank Beckmann
Radio personality, WJR Detroit
Voice of Michigan Football

"*Too many conservatives approach young people with our ideas as if they were spinach — good for you but hard to take. Craig Wieland knows otherwise and in his approach to politics and policy lies much hope that my children and grandchildren will live in an America premised on limited government, individual responsibility, and sensible governance.* "
-Michael Horowitz
Senior Fellow, Hudson Institute
General Counsel, Office of Management and Budget, Reagan Administration

"Pointed Poems *explains the need for business-friendly policies that will create economic growth and does so in a way that anybody can understand, and I mean anybody.*"
-Grover Norquist
Americans for Tax Reform

"*Craig Wieland's new book is chock full of intuitive and entertaining stories that will teach children economic lessons that will prepare them for adult life. Never has the working of the economy been made more accessible, nor the crazy logic of big government advocates more humorous.*"
-Kevin Hassett
Director of Economic Policy Studies and Senior Fellow
American Enterprise Institute

"Pointed Poems *is a comprehensive, thoroughly entertaining means of educating America's next generation on fundamental economic and financial issues. Craig Wieland's Dr. Seuss approach can restore logic and integrity to our future, beginning on the home front.*"
-David L. Littmann
Senior Economist, Mackinac Center for Public Policy

"Craig's book is great stuff. Same value system I have. The book is great for kids and grandkids."
-Mike Ditka
Coach, Chicago Bears

"Don't tell the teachers unions, but all parents know that kids learn more from poems and stories than from textbooks. Craig Wieland is the poet laureate of the Tea Party generation, and his Pointed Poems *should be on every young conservative's bookshelf."*
-Chris Chocola
President, Club for Growth

"If you are like me, you do not want to leave the complete education of your children and grandchildren to a liberal media or progressive professors. Craig's book Pointed Poems *will help you accomplish this. I wish I'd had this book when my children were younger but, thankfully, I have it now for my grandchildren."*
-Lou Holtz
Coach

"Dad, people think conservatives are boring"

"Do you really think that was necessary at the beginning of this book son?"

Before we get started...

This is a provocative book. These are serious matters that we are going to cover. I would like to ask you, the reader, to give the positions outlined herein serious thought and consideration. It is with great apprehension that I address some of the more controversial subjects and I would be disappointed beyond words if I offend anyone with my presentation of the conservative position.

As a conservative, I believe it is important that we listen to all sides of an argument and once we have heard the pros and cons, take a stand. And that's what I have done. Some of these stands will sound harsh, or maybe even unrealistic given the complexity of today's society; but we, as conservatives, must not let our fear of going against the popular view change our fundamental principles. On the other hand, we can't be offensive either. My hope is that if you agree with me, you will do so understanding that many people do not, and we cannot simply ram our ideas down their throats without violating our own principles of humility and civility. Conversely, if you don't agree with the conservative position on any of these subjects, I hope you understand that we are endeavoring to convince you through rational thinking and thoughtful arguments, never by name-calling or with a disrespectful attitude.

America is a great country. In fact, it's exceptionally great, and it is big enough for all sorts of ideas and persuasions. I'm convinced that the conservative one is the right one, but I'm looking forward to the debate, and may the best argument win.

Table of Contents

Chapter   Page

1. The Silver Spoon   10
2. Crime and Poverty   15
3. The Minimum Wage   20
4. Affirmative Action   24
5. Public Education   28
6. Educational Vouchers   31
7. The United Nations and the Bush Doctrine   34
8. The Balanced Budget Amendment   38
9. CAFE Standards   42
10. Prevailing Wages   47
11. Subsidies   51
12. Separation of Church and State   55
13. Property Tax Exemptions for Religious Groups   58
14. Socialism   62
15. Capitalism and Greed   65
16. Israel   69
17. Guns   72
18. Buy American?   76
19. Buy Local!   80
20. Defending Big Salaries   83
21. When Life Begins   86
22. Women's Rights   89
23. Roe Versus Wade   92
24. Marriage   96
25. Pro-Life Guilt   99
26. The Death Penalty   102
27. Climate Change   105
28. Taxes   111
29. Tax Havens   118
30. Tax Fairness   120
31. The Corporate Income Tax   124

32. The Flat Tax   128
33. Economic Incentives   132
34. The Emergency Broadcast System   135
35. National Flood Insurance   137
36. Cash for Clunkers   141
37. Social Security   144
38. Universal Healthcare   147
39. Healthcare Entitlements   151
40. Personal Responsibility   159
41. The Designated Hitter Rule   161
42. Private Courts versus Public Courts   165
43. "Loser Pays" Tort Reform   169
44. Head Start   173
45. Public Funding for Art   175
46. Public Financing for Stadiums   177
47. Eminent Domain   181
48. Environmental Protection   184
49. Public Employee Unions   188
50. The National Labor Relations Board   192
51. The Glass-Steagall Act   196
52. The FDIC   200
53. Banks and "Mark-to-Market"   204
54. Corporate Oversight   208
55. Government Policing of Private Industry   211
56. Campaign Finance Laws   215
57. Free Trade   218
58. English-Only in Public Education   221
59. Printing Money and Inflation   224
60. Taxpayer Funding for The Corporation of PBS   227
61. Rich Guys   229
62. American Exceptionalism   232

Chapter 1

The Silver Spoon

Since we are going to spend the next 61 chapters together, I thought it crucial to provide a quick background of my experience. It underscores the importance of rugged individualism that provides a basis of understanding conservatism.

I was born with a silver spoon in my mouth. There is no doubt about it.

I was also born to a set of poor parents in a mobile home, in the small town of Kawkawlin, Michigan (population 1,200), where the richest guy in town owned the liquor store and it wasn't until I moved away that I discovered he wasn't all that rich after all.

Conventional wisdom says, if you are born into a family that has money, you are given an insurmountable advantage over those who are not. It's my experience that just the opposite is true. That is why a kid who was born in a mobile home, and who moved to a basement house a year later (I actually went down in status after I left the trailer, and that is hard to do!) can confidently claim he was born with a silver spoon in his mouth.

Who gave me this silver spoon? My dad.

My dad started our family construction company, the Wieland-Davco Corporation, the week he returned from the U.S. Army after serving in Korea. He went into the Army as a Private, and he came out a Private. He wasn't decorated or honored in any special way. But to say he wasn't special would be a lie. Donald

Andrew Wieland was special in many ways. Starting a business the same year he married my mom was risky, but he loved taking risks. Having a kid a year later was hard, but he loved hard. Building a construction business in Michigan, at a time when our large companies such as General Motors, Ford, and Chrysler were laying off thousands, made this task more difficult than you can possibly imagine. Doing it all while coaching my little league team, teaching my Sunday school class, and raising a growing family was a sight to behold—and I had a ringside seat.

My dad was successful, but never rich. He worked hard for his money, but it was always tight. It seemed that every time he would make some headway in one area of his business, he would experience a setback in another. How do I know? Because he took me and my brother on business trips with him. I met bankers, suppliers, lawyers, and engineers at a young age. He insisted that my brother and I join him in pouring concrete on jobs when I was not yet a teenager. I saw him smile when he made money. I saw him cry when he was broke. One day when I was twenty-four, my dad said to me, "Son, I want you to be the next president of the Wieland-Davco Corporation," and I did something that I regret to this day—I laughed in his face. "Dad," I said with a sarcastic grin, "the Wieland-Davco Corporation consists of you, me, my brother, and Mom. I'm sorry, Dad, but being president of four people is not really what I want to do." I remember his response: "That's okay, I want you to be president anyway."

One day my dad got sick. Not a "big sick," but something was wrong and we all knew it. Eventually we came to recognize the symptoms of an illness that was never diagnosed as such, but was very similar to Lou Gehrig's disease. Slowly and painfully, he started to waste away in front of our eyes. His construction company by this time had grown to seven people with annual sales of $2 million per year, small by any standard. In 1990, just a few months shy of his 55th birthday, my dad passed away. But before he did, we had a chat.

"Son, I'm pretty lucky," he said. "I'm one of the few people who actually know the approximate time that they are going to die. This gives me time to plan, and here's my plan: I'm not going to leave you any money. Your mom gets it all." And as for the business, he gave me and my brother 10% ownership each. The rest he suggested we could buy from mom, when we had the money. That's it. The 10% ownership, at the time, would not have bought a nice sub-compact car. I had worked at the firm for 14 years, and that was all I got. But was it? Not by a long shot. In retrospect, here's the "silver spoon" my dad gave me.

- **A good name.** After Dad died and I took over the company with my brother, every time we told someone we were Donny Wieland's boys, we always got the benefit of the doubt. We had to prove ourselves for sure, but one thing we didn't have was a lack of credibility. Don Wieland left his boys a good name and that was a huge advantage for us.

- **The knowledge of how to work hard.** Looking back, I can think of how dad planted an acre of pickles in our backyard for us to pick and earn some extra money. This not only kept us busy during our summer vacation, but if you have ever spent some time bending over picking pickles in the hot sun, you know it's hard work. And working with him in the construction field was hard as well. I don't think Dad knew about child labor laws. I don't think he would have cared if he did. He taught us to work hard from a young age, and that gave us a huge advantage as we had to do the same as we grew the firm.

- **To know right from wrong.** Dad taught my Sunday school class. But he wasn't any different at home than he was behind the podium teaching. I saw him in dozens of situations where it would have been easy to cheat just a little to get ahead. But he never did. This sense of right and wrong was consistently enforced. I was told "good job" when I did right, and got a hickory switch to my backside when I chose the opposite. As we grew the business, my brother and I would be faced with many opportunities to bend the law a bit, but Dad would never have stood for it. I think he could still reach my backside, with a long enough hickory switch from heaven.

- **No money.** When my brother and I look back on our business careers, we can honestly say, "We're proud of what we built." Sometimes I see a kid who has been given so much that even if he was wildly successful in his own right; you would have a hard time differentiating his success from what was given to him. Dad had a lot of fun making money, and I just don't think he wanted to deny my brother and me of that kind of fun for ourselves.

So what did I do with this silver spoon I was given? Over the next 25 years we grew the company into one of the larger general contracting firms in the country with offices in four states and annual revenue exceeding $200 million. I'm not bragging, I'm just being honest. I had an incredible advantage over my competition with the silver spoon I was born with.

What does the silver spoon that I was born with have to do with our society today? Everything. Look at the four things dad did for me. Now tell me just one that wouldn't give a kid a great advantage going forward in life. Now show me one that cost my dad a dime. Every parent can do these four things for their kids and in my mind every parent has a responsibility to do so.

"Dad, Tommy's dad doesn't make him work like I have to and he always has lots of money to spend on anything he wants."

"I feel very sorry for Tommy, son."

Chapter 2

Crime and Poverty

- Liberals believe poverty causes crime.
- Conservatives believe crime causes poverty.

My neighborhood is evenly split between conservatives and liberals. At our get-togethers we have lively debates, all in good fun of course, about politics, religion, popular culture and sports. Nothing is off the table, and we have a blast.

On one such evening I asked the question, "If any of you were to open a new business, would you even consider the worst areas of the city of Detroit as a possible location for it?" No one responded positively. I then juiced the pot. "If you could operate there completely tax-free, would you reconsider?" Again, no one said yes.

"Why?" I wanted to know from them, but I already knew the answer in my heart. "It's the crime, isn't it?" The conservatives readily agreed, the liberals reluctantly agreed. No one is going near those places to open a business if they feel unsafe. That sentiment said it all.

Conservatives believe the only way to create wealth is through commerce—the buying and selling of goods and services in the marketplace. Because of this, if commerce is stymied or stopped, the invariable result will be poverty. Conversely, it has been argued—no, taken for granted—that the reverse is true. Poverty causes crime, but personal observation and statistics say otherwise.

Let's start with personal observation. I have been told on numerous occasions that if people are poor, they will steal to support their families, and I believe it. If I was so poor that I could not feed my kids, I would steal to survive. But a person stealing to survive is not what is destroying our urban neighborhoods. That problem is already being addressed by the government in the form of assistance, and by private charities such as food banks and rescue missions. The "fight to survive" type crime that is associated with being poor is not even close to what causes businesses to either leave an area or not enter it in the first place. The type of crime that results in a precipitous drop in commerce resulting in wide-spread poverty is radically different.

And it all starts small. Detroit (and I could use a dozen other examples but I just happen to live near Detroit) didn't become one of the most crime-ridden, poverty-stricken cities in the country overnight. If you drive down Woodward or Jefferson Avenues, you will see grand and beautiful buildings that were built not so very long ago—buildings built by private for-profit companies who saw Detroit as a dynamic and exciting place to live, work, and create a huge amount of wealth. No, Detroit experienced two seemingly small things happening simultaneously, which ultimately destroyed portions this great city. Those two things were the breakdown of the family unit due to a lack of parental responsibility, and broken windows. First, the parents.

It would take a dozen books to explain how or why we have had a shirking of parental responsibility in our urban areas. But no one, not even the most liberal person on the planet, would deny that this a huge issue when it comes to providing good role models for our inner-city kids to follow. If you think I'm being too nuanced, let me be specific: fathers stopped doing their job in the 1960s, and their kids and grandkids have been following their bad examples ever since.

But what about the second thing? Broken windows? In 1972 authors James Wilson and George Kelling wrote a ground-breaking and provocative article in *The Atlantic Monthly* titled, "Broken Windows." The following is an excerpt.

> *Consider a building with a few broken windows. If the windows are not repaired, the tendency is for vandals to break a few more windows. Eventually, they may even break into the building, and if it's unoccupied, perhaps become squatters or light fires inside. Or consider a sidewalk. Some litter accumulates. Soon, more litter accumulates. Eventually, people even start leaving bags of trash from take-out restaurants there or breaking into cars.*

This article points out that most crimes start small. Notice how the two examples cited start with something as innocuous as "breaking a few more windows" and ends up with arson. Or "some more litter accumulates" and ends up with breaking into cars. Just as gasoline doesn't burn on its own and a lit match is arguably harmless, put them both together and you can have an explosion big enough to destroy huge parts of a city. And that's exactly what has happened. Fathers stopped disciplining their kids for breaking a few windows and throwing a bit of trash around. This happened because their own self-destructive behavior practiced elsewhere in their lives did not give them the moral authority in the family to do so. At the same time, police departments were too busy to bother with a few broken windows or littering laws. Little by little, dads had kids who followed in their footsteps, and cops kept letting the little things slide. Sixty years later, we have rampant crime in our urban centers and somehow we blame it on being poor. Don't insult poor people. Don't confuse them with nor associate them with thugs. The fact is, millions of people today are poor because no one will come to their neighborhoods and take the risk to start businesses and create wealth. Entrepreneurs don't take this risk because they don't want to get robbed or shot—and when they stay away, people become poor. Cause and effect. It might not be politically correct to say this, but it's true.

But is it true in reverse? What if crime dropped dramatically? We have a prime example of that as well. Heather MacDonald writing in an August 2012 article for *The Wall Street Journal* observed:

> *"Crime in New York City has dropped 80% since the early 1990s (under Mayor Giuliani), a decline unmatched anywhere in the country. The change has yielded an explosion of commerce in once forlorn neighborhoods, a boom in tourism, and a sharp rise in property values. Nowhere was the effect more dramatic than in the city's poorest areas.*
>
> *When the bullets stopped flying, entrepreneurs snapped up the vacant lots that had served as breeding grounds of crime. Senior citizens were*

able to visit friends without fear of getting mugged. Children could sleep in their own beds rather than in bathtubs, no longer needing shelter from stray gunfire. Target, Home Depot and other national chains moved into thoroughfares long ruled by drug gangs, providing jobs for local workers and giving residents retail choices taken for granted in middle-class neighborhoods.

Most significant, more than 10,000 Black and Hispanic males avoided the premature death that would have been their fate had New York's homicide rate remained at its early pre-1990s apex. Blacks and Hispanics have made up 79% of the decline in homicide victims since 1993.

Conservatives believe that crime causes poverty, and crime is the result of the lack of parents taking responsibility to raise their kids properly, combined with police departments not being able to protect citizens anymore. What method did Mayor Giuliani employ to get the cops to do their job? He started by telling them that breaking any law was a crime and it should be prosecuted, right down to punks breaking windows.

Chapter 3

The Minimum Wage

Conservatives believe that minimum wage laws are wrong on many different levels and actually do more harm than good to the groups they are trying to help. As many other government mandates have unintended consequences, this one is no different. Similarly, like all federal mandates, once they are started, they are nearly impossible to kill off. And finally (and this is where conservatives really get steamed), the people who have caused the problem—in this case liberal politicians— demand that they be treated like heroes for advocating on behalf of the poor against greedy business owners. Now for a reality check.

There is an old saying that goes something like this: "*If you want less of something, tax it.*" In other words, make it more expensive. For instance, the government wanted to reduce the number of people who smoked cigarettes, so they raised the tax on them so high that millions of people decided it just wasn't worth the price to smoke anymore. This happens in the private sector as well. When companies want to keep their products "exclusive" or "elite," they raise its price so fewer people buy it—giving those who *do* buy it the feeling of being "special."

Unfortunately this has been the unintended consequence resulting from mandating a minimum wage. We get fewer workers—and in times like these, that's exactly the opposite of what we need.

As stated previously, conservatives oppose minimum wage mandates on many different levels, but let's start with the first one. They believe that government has no business dictating to a private company how much they should pay workers. This goes from how high they can pay them, to how low they can pay them. Some courts have disagreed with this principle, but conservatives long ago realized that sometimes there is a difference between being legal and being a good practice.

Second, it may seem to some people that it is necessary for the government to protect the poor and vulnerable from the exploitation that invariably would arise if a minimum wage was not mandated, but that is simply not true. In a capitalist, free-market society such as we enjoy in the U.S., workers are free to do one of three things. 1.) They can form unions and bargain collectively. Now I realize that the jobs usually subjected to the minimum wage mandate are not ones that are typically unionized, but what unions in general do is put upward pressure on employers everywhere to pay all employees more, or they (the employers) run the risk of further unionization. 2.) If workers feel they need more pay, they can quit their jobs and move to where they are paid more. My construction company for example, is constantly monitoring the marketplace for two things: A) how much are job candidates being offered from our competitors, and B) how much do we need to pay our existing employees to keep them at our company? 3.) And this has more to do with our welfare state than the free market: workers who don't feel they are being paid enough can stay home. Given the myriad of government programs offering assistance to those who are out of work, private businesses have to compete not only with one another, but with the government as well. The phenomenon of providing such a strong safety net for the lowest paid workers that it actually competes with employers for lower wage employees is rarely discussed when the welfare programs are adopted. The attention is on helping people. The unintended consequence is that these same people can choose not to go to work, and businesses suffer when the labor pool is reduced.

Third, the government should not artificially and indiscriminately establish the minimum value that a person is worth in terms of dollars per hour. In 2012, the time of this writing, that figure was $7.25. During some of the original debates regarding the government's belief that a minimum wage would help raise workers' standard of living, one conservative responded with a sarcastic, "Well, why put it low then—let's really help them out and make it $100 an hour." He was accused of being insensitive and not serious. (That kind of response usually comes when an opponent doesn't have a good answer.) Staying with the danger of establishing the worth of a person as a minimum of $7.25 per hour, the problem is that some people are not worth $7.25 per hour, and if they aren't, businesses can't hire them. I know it sounds crass, but the worth of a person is not established by the government—it's determined by what skills they have, how much they know, and how hard they are willing to work. Some people lack in one, two, or perhaps all three of these areas. They *are* employable; it's just that it's not worth it to the employer to pay them $7.25 per hour, so they don't. That person works for the competition instead—in this case, the government— who pays them to stay home. Why doesn't this person apply for a job at a different business or industry? The result would be the same. Markets are efficient, and over time the amount a person is paid is exactly what they are worth. If they are worth less than $7.25 per hour, they don't get hired.

Fourth, the jobs the minimum wage is usually intended for were never meant to be permanent careers for anyone. Working behind a counter at a fast-food restaurant is great, but in almost all cases, it is an entry-level position, allowing a person to experience the work environment, make a little money, and start to build a resume. The sad truth is, businesses could employ a lot more people for these types of jobs if they didn't have to pay the minimum wage, and if the government stopped competing against them by offering an option to stay home.

But conservatives are pragmatic and we have to tell the truth. Our society is in desperate need of jobs but has to deal with the reality that hundreds of thousands of people don't have jobs today because politicians, feigning to be their "friends," are trying to protect them from themselves—falsely telling them that if they don't get $7.25 per hour, they should stay home. With friends like that, who needs enemies?

In conclusion; if you want fewer workers, make employers pay more for hiring them. Who would want fewer workers? Nobody, but that's what happens. This is the unintended consequence of politicians mandating that all employers, public and private, pay more for a worker than what they may be worth.

Chapter 4

Affirmative Action

Someone once said that in the end, treason is just a matter of dates. For example, loyal British subjects living in the American colonies were on the side of the government on July 3rd, 1776. The next day these same people would be seen as guilty of treason by the newly-formed United States government. What changed? Well, there comes a time in every great struggle when the old is pushed aside to make way for the new.

How does this relate to affirmative action? Because it's time to do away with the old and usher in the new. Conservatives believe that all people in this country should be judged solely and exclusively on their character and actions, and never on their skin color. This will not happen until affirmative action laws are abolished. In the meantime, millions of hardworking people of color are living with the fact their leaders such as Jesse Jackson, Al Sharpton, and Louis Farrakhan are demanding that they trade their self-respect for the false promise of the advantages of preferential treatment.

As mentioned, one of the foundational principles of conservatism is the belief that every person is primarily responsible for his or her own actions, and the subsequent results of these actions. From this principle, many other beliefs grow, including positions on limited government, self-reliance, environmental responsibility, and parenting responsibilities. However, for this fundamental principle of personal responsibility to be enacted on a national scale, something must happen first. The black community as a whole must demand that its leaders quit advocating for the preferential treatment of their race, and start insisting that society judge them the same way everyone else is judged. That is, individually, by the results of their decisions.

In the landmark Supreme Court decision of 2003, which challenged the University of Michigan's use of racial preferences in admission decisions, Justice Sandra Day O'Conner said that affirmative action is still needed in America, but hoped that its days were numbered. She stated, "We expect that 25 years from now, the use of racial preferences will not be necessary to further the interest approved today."

As of the time of this writing, this gives us 16 years.

First, as a conservative, I disagree with Justice O'Conner, but I'm not a Supreme Court judge. If she says we need this program for an additional 16 years, I have no choice but to wait. But it's interesting to me that what she didn't say might have been more important than what she did say. She didn't say, *"I'm sending a warning to the leaders of the black community. You guys better understand that the number of days in which you can keep your people from believing that their success might be due to some government program and not their own talent and hard work are numbered."*

But she didn't—so I will. The black community is no different from any other group of people sharing something in common. Protestants, Boy Scouts, golf leagues, unions, charities, book clubs, gay men—you name it, all share some value or attribute that unites them, and they all have leaders, some elected and others just recognized. Unfortunately for the black community, their recognized leaders are failing them miserably. My evidence for this is empirical. Since that day in 2003 when the Supreme Court issued its verdict, I have heard precious few warnings come from these leaders regarding the eventual phasing-out of affirmative action programs. I haven't heard them voicing their concern that people of color prepare themselves for this event. And I haven't heard them agree with the observation that Justice O'Conner made. No, in fact I have heard just the opposite. Every time there is an opportunity to point out that our society is racially stacked against them, they do. Every opportunity to divide us along color lines is taken and exploited. Every microphone available to them is used to reinforce that their people are being taken advantage of and justice needs to be served. In the meantime millions of black people who would love to tell them to shut up don't feel they can because they will be seen as somehow "siding with the opponent." This was recently evidenced by the icy reception given to both author Juan Williams and actor Bill Cosby when they had the audacity to challenge this overt manipulation by the leaders of their race.

These leaders are not saying that affirmative action programs should continue indefinitely. They know they can't advocate for that because it would be too obvious, too blatant, and too indefensible in the public arena. No, they are being more clever than that. By continuing to cry about inequality, racism, and the lack of opportunity their people have, this will become a self-fulfilling prophecy. If their people believe this dangerous rhetoric, then sure enough when the 16 years are over, they will still feel they need more time.

I am a white man, but I'm not blind and deaf. I see this happening, and I hear from many of my friends in the black community and they are sickened by this as well.

Conservatives believe in giving people a helping hand when they are down. We do this out of a deep respect that we have for our fellow man and we know, as well as the next person, that sometimes compensation is necessary to help "right" wrongs that have occurred in the past. But the time for affirmative action programs to end is coming, and when it does, we don't want to have to look like the "bad guys" anymore.

"Hate and hurt are on a roll here in America! If what was happening here was happening in South Africa, it'd be called racist apartheid. If it was happening in Germany, we'd call it Nazism. And in Italy, we'd call it fascism. Here we call it conservatism." **(Jesse Jackson in a speech following a GOP political victory)**

Chapter 5

Public Education

Conservatives believe that the public education system is just one of the many forms of schooling that are appropriate for the education of our children. I am a third-generation conservative. My grandfather, father, and I all went to the Bay City public schools in Michigan. My wife (who attended Peoria public schools in Illinois) and I chose to send our five daughters to the Okemos public schools in Michigan. Our oldest two grandsons attend the Blacksburg public schools in Virginia. In each of these cases the education we received or are receiving was adequate and complete. But this does not mean that conservatives believe the public school system, in every case, is the right choice. Many times it is not.

Conservatives will support their local public schools as long as the product they are producing (smart, well-adjusted kids, ready to enter society) is worth the price they are paying. When the quality of the product slips, they can do one of two things— work to change the system, or go to a competitor. When I was a kid, parents almost always did the former. I couldn't begin to count the number of times my mom visited the school to partake in PTA meetings, teacher conferences, and other school-centered gatherings. My dad chaperoned a field trip to Tiger Stadium once and I count that day as one of the greatest days of my life as I was able to see my boyhood hero Al Kaline play right field. My parents and those of my friends were actively involved in our school system and were its biggest cheerleaders. I can still remember my mom pleading with friends and neighbors to pass the local school millage, because she knew how important it was to the quality of our education. Finally, I can remember the aforementioned parent-teacher conferences when almost without exception, every parent showed up, and every kid knew they would.

Today, when a parent has his or her kids in a public school system and the quality of the product slips, the first choice (to change the system) is seldom even a remote possibility. When they go to the school, they see kids who are unruly and rude to their teachers and administrators. They see kids dressed in black called "Goths" who by all rights may be good kids, but they sure look scary. They see graffiti written on walls using foul or coarse language and finally, they see an overall lack of an environment that would foster good learning. When it comes to parental involvement, many times there is none.

> Note: My daughter, Wendy, taught in a public school for a short time after college. One day she told me that she and a few of her fellow teachers were going to go to Detroit the next day (a Friday) to do some shopping. I inquired as to why they were going on a school day and her reply shocked me. "Well, last year I sat in the room alone all day and not one parent showed up for parent-teacher conferences. This was the same for the other teachers, so this year we are going shopping instead." She had no concern that even one parent would show up.

So, instead of attempting the impossible and trying to change the system, more and more parents are opting for the competition, including private, parochial, charter, or home schools. The sad thing is, they will still be required to pay their taxes to the public school system, even though they choose not to send their kids there. Think about that for a moment. Parents are so adamantly opposed to sending their kids into this system that they would rather pay double and send their kids elsewhere.

> Note #2. Just down the road from where my daughter taught was a charter school. This school consistently ranked among the top schools in the area, public or private. The socio-economic makeup of the students came from the surrounding neighborhood and was exactly the same as my daughter's school. One day I had the opportunity to talk with the administrator. "What is your secret?" I asked. Without hesitation he stated, "Parental involvement and personal responsibility." When asked to elaborate he basically told me that every parent must spend a minimum of time at the school volunteering. If they don't their kid has to leave. In addition to this, if a student consistently misses homework assignments, they will be asked to leave as well.

There are thousands of great public schools in this country; but without the ability of the administrations to enforce discipline, unions that defend poor teachers, parents who don't support the schools, and the availability of other great options, the future of public schools does not look good.

Chapter 6

Educational Vouchers

Albert Einstein said, "Insanity is doing what you've always done, but somehow expecting different results." Nowhere is this more evident than in the mindset of the person defending how our urban public school systems are being operated today. Conservatives believe that if the parents of the kids who were attending these schools were to be given vouchers to use at any recognized system of learning, they then would have the power to immediately provide their kids with the best education possible. Conservatives also believe that this would overwhelmingly help poor and disadvantaged families who don't have the means to choose, over rich ones who have plenty of options. What is baffling to us is why we seem to be standing alone on this issue. Where are the traditional advocates for the poor on this one? You'll have to ask them.

I won't go into my defense of public schools. I've already covered that in the previous chapter. Suffice it to say, I am a third generation attendee of public schools, my five daughters went to public schools, and my oldest two grandsons go to public schools. But all public schools are not equal. Not by a long shot. Our local public school ranked third in the state of Michigan on a whole list of important tests. That's third overall, *including* private, parochial, and charter schools. Don't tell conservatives that public schools can't compete, because they know they can. But conservatives are pragmatists. We deal with the facts as they are, not as we would like them to be. And the fact is, a preponderance of the public schools, in our urban areas, are failing miserably in educating our kids. Every year we hear from the leaders of these schools how things are "turning around," whatever that means. If they aren't improving we hear that they are working on a plan to improve. If a critic points out their failures, invariably they are told it's due to conditions out of their control—but if they had more funding, things would "turn around."

It's time to stop the insanity. Things are not "turning around" in our nation's urban public schools. They are getting worse. Let's try something new. Let's give the parents or legal guardians of these urban public school children vouchers worth about $8,000 each school year. Let them take their vouchers to any school they want, or home school if they wish, and let's get those kids out of these under-performing, gang-threatened, violence-filled excuses called urban public schools now!

I can hear the liberal argument a mile away. *"We can't give our tax dollars to parochial schools. They might teach the kids religious things that their parents don't agree with!"* Don't let them do that. Don't let them change the subject. No one suggested that we force parents to put their kids in a school that would violate their religious principles, but they could if they wanted to. And that is the freedom they would have as parents with vouchers. Money is no longer a concern. They can look at the local public school, the private school a few miles away, the Catholic school around the corner, or the charter school that has moved in because they see the opportunity that has arisen. In the end, if they find that the local Catholic school is the best alternative for them, even if they aren't Catholic, they can choose to send their kids there. If they want to continue to send their kids to the public school, that's their prerogative as well. What will happen to the urban public schools if this happens? I think we all know the answer to that. It should have happened when the first kid brought that gun or knife to school years ago. It should have happened when the administrators were not allowed to fire bad teachers. It should have happened when the principal was no longer allowed to discipline the kids. It should have happened when the gangs showed up, and drug dealing was done on the sidewalk out front. It should have happened when the dropout rate hit 50%. It should have happened a long time ago, but finally with vouchers maybe it will.

Conservatives believe in a limited role for government. We are the first ones to voice concern when we see our tax dollars going to waste such as they are in the urban public schools. But we know the way to change the government is through the spread of knowledge and elections. It is our hope as conservatives that the spread of knowledge regarding the use of vouchers to help solve our urban public school catastrophe will result in electing leaders who have the fortitude to demand this change.

The kids and their parents caught in this trap called urban public schools are crying for help. Let's give it to them.

Chapter 7

The United Nations and The Bush Doctrine

These two subjects could each stand on their own but like a good cigar and a glass of Scotch; they go a lot better together.

Conservatives believe that the United Nations, while far from perfect, does a great deal of good around the world, and that the United States should be actively engaged in its activities. Conservatives also believe that there are times when it is in the best interest of the United States to act unilaterally in defending ourselves in crisis, or (and here's the Bush Doctrine) to act proactively if we are threatened with harm.

The United Nations was founded in 1945, as a successor to the League of Nations, to stop wars between countries, and to provide a platform for dialogue. It contains multiple subsidiary organizations to carry out its missions. These subsidiary organizations are where the work gets done, or in the case of the Security Council, where it doesn't. They are as follows;

- **The General Assembly**: The General Assembly is the main deliberative body of the United Nations and meets in regular yearly sessions. Over a two-week period at the start of each session, all members have the opportunity to address the assembly. Traditionally, the Secretary-General makes the first statement, followed by the President of the assembly. This is where presidents and dictators from around the world are treated alike. This is where Nikita Khrushchev, then leader of the Soviet Union, took off his shoe and banged it on the podium to make his silly point. This is where Hugo Chavez, following an address by the United States President, George W. Bush, said he smelled the burning sulfur of hell as the devil had just left the room. This is the room where Colonel Kaddafi and Mahmoud Ahmadinejad spewed their hate and lies. Yep, the General Assembly is a great platform to see what the rest of the world thinks of the United States, Israel, and western democracy in general. We get a ringside seat because it all happens in New York City.

- **The Security Council**: The Security Council is charged with maintaining peace and security among countries. While other divisions of the U.N. can only make suggestions to its member governments, the Security Council can make binding decisions that its members have agreed to carry out. The decisions are known as U.N. Security Council Resolutions. Unlike the General Assembly, the Security Council is made up of 15 members with five of them being permanent and ten non-permanent. Now here's the rub. The five permanent members each hold veto power, allowing them to block any resolution that they do not agree with. These five members are the United States, Russia, China, France, and the United Kingdom. Conservatives have no problem with the Security Council per se. It's just that 99% of the time, these five countries cannot reach agreement on even the most obvious response to atrocities being perpetrated by evil tyrants. For example, at the time of this writing, Syria's President, Bashar Al Assad, is killing tens of thousands of his own citizens using the Syrian military to bomb residential areas in cities throughout the country. The United States has tried on numerous occasions to get the Security Council to punish this butcher with brutal sanctions and/or other punitive measures, but have been repeatedly blocked by Russia and China.

- **The Secretariat:** The U.N. Secretariat is headed by the Secretary General who is assisted by staff worldwide. This division of the U.N. is where the studies come from—studies that are used by the rest of the U.N. bodies for the work they do. It is also charged with carrying out the tasks as directed by the other U.N. divisions such as the aforementioned General Assembly or Security Council. Finally, it is charged with helping to resolve international disputes, peace-keeping operations, and organizing conferences.
- **The International Court of Justice:** The International Court of Justice, located in The Hague, Netherlands, is the primary judicial division of the U.N. Its purpose is to adjudicate disputes among its member states.
- **The Economic and Social Council:** The Economic and Social Council assists the General Assembly by promoting economic and social cooperation and development.

The United Nations, as a whole, is a worthwhile organization. If it didn't exist, something else would have to take its place, and that something else could be a lot less friendly to the United States. However, conservatives believe we should support the United Nations for reasons other than the good it may do around the world. The U.N. gives the United States a platform to explain to the world what our intentions are, and to seek approval. If we receive such approval, as in the case of the Iraq War, we then have the legitimate reason to proceed with our intentions. If we don't receive approval, the President of the

United States can forthrightly declare, *"We tried, and they wouldn't listen. Now I am going to act unilaterally to protect the interests of the United States."* This position is defensible, due to the extreme difficulty of getting the Security Council to pass even the most obvious of resolutions.

Now, here is where the Bush Doctrine comes in and why it's so important. Up until 2002, the United States was seen as a country that reacted to situations in the world once an act of terror or war had taken place. Retaliation for harm perpetrated on us was our standard position. But in 2002, President George W. Bush raised the bar. He declared that the United States, from that point on, was going to have the prerogative to operate pro-actively—disarming, killing, or destroying our enemies if we felt it was in our best interest to do so. No, we wouldn't go to the U.N. to ask permission for these covert operations. If we did, this would tip our hand to our enemies, thus thwarting our efforts. Instead, we were going to retain the right to go after our enemies, before they come after us.

Conservatives believe that the Bush Doctrine finally puts the world back in balance. The U.S. can, and will, use the United Nations and the platform it provides, to explain our positions and ask for assistance. If the U.S. gets this assistance, great. If it doesn't, then that's okay too. The U.S. refuses to give up its right as a sovereign nation to determine its own destiny. The U.S. won't turn its foreign policy decisions over to the United Nations. They are a good organization that does some good things and the U.S. is glad to pay over 20% of its budget, even though it makes up 5% of the world's population—but the U.S. is the U.S.: part of, but not beholden to, the U.N.

Chapter 8

The Balanced Budget Amendment

Hold on to your hats—I'm warning you, this is going to get rough.

Conservatives are pragmatic. They deal with the facts as they are, not as they would like them to be. And because of this, they are opposed to an amendment to the Constitution requiring a balanced budget.

If you are willing to listen to my logic, I would be more than pleased. If you just throw this book in the trash, I completely understand. This isn't going to be easy for any of us.

In the beginning, when the original framers drafted the Constitution, they made arrangements for budgets to be submitted and debated. Spending bills that reflected those budgets were then passed and signed into law. But what they did *not* do is establish the accounting procedures that should have accompanied that spending. They simply looked at government spending as money-in (taxes) and money-out (expenditures) on an annual basis. This may work for a shoe shop or candy store, but it is woefully inadequate for a nation.

The basic problem with this accounting method is that it doesn't allow for a capital account. In other words, there is no place to account for capital assets to be allocated. Let me ask you a question. How much is Yellowstone National Park worth? You have no idea, and neither do I. The reason we don't know is that there is no ledger being kept in Washington that accounts for all of the assets the United States has purchased over the past 236 years. NASA, the Washington Monument, the interstate highway system, the White House, the Public Broadcasting System, Isle Royale (that's here in Michigan), and the Everglades are but a tiny fraction of the things that the government has bought in the past, and they expensed the purchase in the year it was made. Unfortunately, they treated items with little or no lasting value (such as a utility bill) the same as ones *with* value (such as a national park). The first rule of accounting—keep accurate records of what you own—has not been followed.

On the other hand, we *do* have a liability account. Today it stands at $16 trillion. But this account is terribly flawed. It only reflects what we borrowed in the past. It does not account for the cost of benefits, or entitlements, which will be coming due in the future.

These two fundamental accounting tools that every business in the country would deem absolutely essential—knowing what you own and knowing what you owe—are missing from the debate, or are hopelessly flawed. Now let's look at the ramifications of this as it relates to the Balanced Budget Amendment.

On its surface, conservatives would strongly believe that the federal government should balance its budget every year. This almost goes without saying, but since they oppose the Balanced Budget Amendment, I feel compelled to reiterate this fact. Conservatives are fiscal hawks. They despise wasteful spending. They want the government to live within its means. The very word "conservative" speaks of caution and prudence. Of course they want a balanced budget.

But the fact is, even if we don't know what we own and the value of it, we do know what we owe. And it's not what is down on paper. The aforementioned $16 trillion is the total amount of the outstanding debt today. That is a fraction of what we owe. Because of the promises (entitlements) made to our citizens by reckless politicians in the past, the net present value of these benefits—mainly from Medicaid, Medicare, and Social Security—is a whopping $45 trillion. Add this to the $16 trillion and it's over $60 trillion. For those of you who like big numbers that's $60,000,000,000,000. To put it another way, it's sixty thousand billion.

Conservatives believe in "limited" government, but we do believe in some government. We believe that it should protect us from enemies, both foreign and domestic. We believe it should protect our food supply, build our infrastructure, and prosecute criminals. We believe that these basic functions of the government are so important, that they should take precedence over the entitlement programs mentioned above and the hundreds of programs that, while not labeled "entitlements," are probably not absolutely essential to the basic functions that a government must perform. In other words: nice to have, if you've got the money.

The problem with the Balanced Budget Amendment is that all spending will be equal, and the indisputable fundamental role of government as briefly outlined above will be subject to the "meat cleaver" along with the entitlement programs that are the core reason we have these huge deficits in the first place. As conservatives, we would rather suffer the consequences of more debt (runaway inflation and loss of credit being just two) than weaken our national defense to the point where we are vulnerable to attacks from our enemies, foreign and—as unfortunately is the case lately—domestic.

We have a huge problem in this country. We elect politicians to make the hard choices that they said they wanted to make when they ran for office. They can start with the next budget and make structural changes to the entitlement programs that will bring them under control in the near future if they had the guts to do it. If they do this and, by doing so, get us back on track fiscally, then by all means, yes, let's amend the Constitution to require that we balance the budget every year so we never get into this situation again. But doing so now will result in these same politicians arguing that hip replacements for 90-year-olds should stay, and a new destroyer or attack helicopter must go.

By the way, maybe we should put someone in charge of starting a capital account. If we had one, we could start a national dialog about selling some of these assets to finance our entitlements. I would just love to see the liberals have to decide between adding another benefit, and selling Grand Teton National Park to pay for it. My guess is that they might just decide to drop the idea of the new benefit altogether.

Support for the Balanced Budget Amendment is easy to put on a bumper sticker and pretend that it will cure what ails us, but it won't. Subjecting our national security to the hope that the politicians might protect us from our enemies is not a risk conservatives are willing to take.

Chapter 9

CAFE Standards

If you live near Detroit, as I do, you know what CAFE standards are. If you live somewhere else, you might think it's a rating system for small restaurants. Actually, I wish the government would have gotten into the business of rating small cafes instead; it couldn't possibly have the negative effect in the marketplace that the real CAFE standards are about to have.

Rahm Emanuel, now the mayor of the great city of Chicago, once said "Never let a serious crisis go to waste." He understood what conservatives have known for a long time— that in a serious crisis people will make decisions that they wouldn't ordinarily make, and any politician worth his salt should take advantage of the situation. This is exactly what has happened with CAFE standards (which, by the way, stands for Corporate Average Fuel Economy).

In 1973, the United States was in a crisis. Eight years earlier the Organization of the Petroleum Exporting Countries (OPEC) formed a cartel that included twelve nations who wanted to control the level of production and the price of oil. These nations were predominately Muslim, and when a coalition of Arab States led by Egypt and Syria attacked Israel on Yom Kippur (the most sacred day of the Jewish year), OPEC played the "oil weapon" to punish Israel and its supporters, including the United States. This was done by imposing an embargo on shipping oil to countries that supported Israel, causing the price of oil on the world market to skyrocket.

As with most crises, this one passed. But to borrow from the words of Mayor Emanuel, Congress just couldn't let this crisis go to waste. They decided to wrap themselves up in the American flag and proclaim that it was for the good of the country to fight back against OPEC. They turned to their own auto industry and unilaterally forced them to build cars that got a minimum of 18 miles per gallon. With the Arab oil embargo fresh on our minds, we, the American people, made a rash decision. We allowed this governmental intrusion into private American business to stand. The camel got its nose under the tent that day, and thirty years later the federal government now _owns_ large portions of the auto industry—but that is another lesson for another time. Back to the CAFE.

Like most government programs, they start out small and innocuous. This one only applied to passenger cars, and it was only 18 mpg. It seemed like a small price to pay for the feeling that we were somehow fighting back against OPEC. Few suggested that we should let the market deal with this problem. OPEC was our enemy and we had to fight them. At the time, our president was Jimmy Carter. Along with telling the auto companies how to build their cars; he lowered the speed limit on the federal highways to 55 mph, and asked everyone to voluntarily lower their thermostats in their homes and offices. All this was done as a way of fighting back. No one suggested that perhaps we should just drill and extract more oil.

In 1979, Congress added pickup trucks to the list. The automakers balked, pointing out trucks (being larger than cars) get lower gas mileage. So to compromise a bit they lowered the combined average to 17.2 mpg. Congress got what it wanted though; an expanded federal program.

In 1984 the number was 20. In 2007 the number was 22. By 2011 it was 24.

But wait a minute, when was the last time you have even heard of OPEC? I thought this whole government mandate was to fight back against their high oil prices? Nope, when the OPEC threat went away, the government very slowly and very quietly changed its tune. With the price of oil now in check due to the efficiency of markets and new discoveries here at home and in friendly countries such as Great Britain, Canada, and Norway, the chances of the U.S. getting harmed by another OPEC embargo is significantly reduced. But in the mind of the government, this crisis was not going to be wasted. No, instead of saying to the auto companies, "OK, you guys are now free to build and sell what the market wants to buy," it pointed to evidence of global warming—and by linking this phenomenon to carbon dioxide—created by automobiles, said we needed the program now more than ever. What???

Armed with this new reason to impose federally mandated minimum MPG standards, the president has recently announced that the new CAFE standard for 2025 (just 13 years away) will be a whopping 54.5 miles per gallon.

John O'Dell, writing a recent article for Edmond.com, pointed out how this new mandate will affect consumers.

- The cost of buying new cars and trucks will go up. Prices are certain to climb because of the cost of the new technologies needed to comply with the rules. Those technologies include everything from turbochargers and new generations of multispeed automatic transmissions to battery-electric powertrains. What happens when the cost of something goes up? You sell fewer of them, and the jobs associated with building fewer vehicles are lost as well.

- Your choice at the dealership will go down. There will likely be more hybrids to choose among, but fewer trucks.

- Overall vehicle operating costs will go up. Insurance costs could rise, both because of the increased cost of cars and the anticipated hike in collision repair costs associated with the greater use of the plastics, lightweight alloys and aluminum necessary for lighter, more fuel-efficient vehicles.

- Safety will be a concern. The use of weight-saving materials will not only affect repair costs but could make newer vehicles more susceptible to damage in collisions with older, heavier vehicles, especially SUVs and pickups. Their occupants could be at a safety disadvantage.

- The cost of fuel and the possibility of new taxes to replace lost fuel tax revenue are very likely. If vehicles use half the amount of fuel than they used to, the gas tax will have to double to get the same revenue.

Conservatives believe that when the government intrudes into the marketplace, as it has with the CAFE standards, the unintended consequences are enormous. In the end, our automakers will be forced into making cars that consumers don't want, at prices they can't afford. The governmental solution to that problem is already coming into view. They will use taxpayers' dollars to subsidize the purchase of these vehicles, basically bribing you to buy them. The current bribe to buy a Chevy Volt is $7,500.

And all because a bunch of Arabs attacked Israel 40 years ago.

Chapter 10

Prevailing Wages

Conservatives believe that when someone works for the government, they should not be entitled to get more money than if they worked for the private sector. Yet, on any given day, hundreds of thousands of carpenters, laborers, steel workers, brick masons, and backhoe operators get just that. The fact that the government would demand that private companies, who work on government projects, charge higher prices than what they normally would get defies logic and is reprehensible.

The current prevailing wage laws mandating this requirement stem from what is known as the Davis-Bacon Act, signed into law in 1931. Passed by a Republican Congress and signed by a Republican President, this law offers empirical evidence that the words "Republican" and "Conservative" are by no means synonymous.

Eighty years ago, a Republican Congressman from New York, Robert Bacon, brought some pork home to his district—a new Veterans Administration hospital. Knowing that he could take a lot of credit for directing federal taxpayer dollars to his area, he was proud to be seen as the "sugar daddy." But then the free enterprise system kicked in and the contractor hired workers from Alabama to construct some of the project. The workers from Alabama paid taxes, followed the rules, and did a good job. The only problem was that they weren't from New York and this didn't sit very well with Congressman Bacon. I wasn't there so I don't know exactly what happened, but I'll bet my last dollar that Congressman Bacon grabbed some cigars and headed for a backroom, muttering, "This must be stopped." Meeting a fellow Republican, James Davis from Pennsylvania, having the same concern, they decided to make the taxpayer pay, and pay dearly.

Again, I wasn't around eighty years ago. It was a different time, and I suppose there might have been some logic to the argument that local politicians should get the credit for local jobs "created" when they brought home the bacon on public works projects; but it seems to me something else could have been suggested by these guys to do the trick. Maybe big signs on the projects with their pictures and names on them would have been enough, or maybe naming the bridge, road, building or sewage treatment plant (oh, that would be ironic) after them could have given them the credit they craved for spending the taxpayers money the way they did. But instead, they forced all contractors nationwide to pay higher wages on any federally-funded project, with the logic that "out of towners" would have the field leveled for them. This would also discourage contractors from taking advantage of workers who would be willing to travel, taking a little less in wages at the same time.

By enacting the Davis-Bacon law, legislators got a "twofer" (this is a phenomenon whereby a person buys one thing but gets a second added benefit at no extra cost). As with every government solution, there are always unintended consequences and this added benefit was the bureaucracy that was now needed to monitor the wages of every area of the country to determine what the "prevailing" wage is, along with the responsibility of insuring compliance with the law. Think... thousands of federal workers are now employed by the U.S.

Department of Labor, costing the taxpayers additional millions of dollars over and above the cost of the "prevailing wage."

Critics have argued that if workers were paid a lower wage, that somehow quality and safety would be jeopardized but that simply isn't true. Every government project has representatives, either from the government agency the work is being done for or outside construction managers, who are responsible for quality assurance on these jobs. In regards to safety, each state has an agency looking after construction safety and then there is OSHA operating on a federal level. No, the critics are wrong. Paying workers less than the prevailing wage does not allow the contractors to diminish safety or quality one bit.

Conservatives are pragmatic and we deal with the facts. The fact is that today's construction workers are highly-skilled, competent, and very well-trained. This applies to union and non-union companies. There is no need to "protect" the worker against exploitation because the situation in the real world is this: if you are a skilled construction worker, your employer does not want to lose your talent to the competition. They will pay you for your services commensurate to your worth; and this will result in the best workers getting higher wages and the slackers getting less. That's how the free market works. To demand that the taxpayer subsidize the slacker so that he is paid what a local union worker gets is unfair and not logical. I'm in the construction business and I see this every day.

Conservatives believe that the free market should determine the wages paid to construction workers, whether they are on a taxpayer-funded public project or a new home, built for a growing family.

I'll make another wager. When Mr. Bacon and Mr. Davis spent their own money building their own homes, I'll bet they went with the lowest qualified bid and didn't give one thought as to what the chosen contractor was paying his workers. They would have surmised, and rightly so, that this was his own business. Conservatives wish they would have given the contractors on federally-funded projects the same consideration.

Chapter 11

Subsidies

Conservatives believe that subsidies provided by the government to businesses and consumers are wrong, economically harmful, disruptive to the marketplace—but great for politics. Politicians of every political stripe howl against them in general, but vote for them anytime the recipient can either support them, or send in a big contribution. Subsidies have made hypocrites of the most conservative politicians, and it's time someone speaks truth to power.

When the average person thinks or hears about subsidies, they think about "big corporations" or "fat cats" getting millions of dollars from the government; just making the rich richer. While there is plenty of this happening for sure, subsidies are so prevalent in our political system that the average Joe is getting them, and doesn't even know it. Now, you may be thinking to yourself, "Well, if everyone else is getting something for nothing, I should get a little piece of the pie too." You might be tempted to think that way, but subsidies, like all "free lunches," usually come with a price. What if you found out how much the government is giving out in subsidies to average folks like you and me? Well, here's a sampling:

- If you have a mortgage, the interest you pay is tax deductible. The government has subsidized home owners with this deduction to the tune of $443 billion over the past 4 years.

- Did you pay property taxes on your house? They are deductible as well. The subsidy to those of us who own homes and paid property taxes was $112 billion over the past four years.
- Now, I understand that you are probably a good person and, as such, like to do good things for disadvantaged people. However, every time you give a dime, the amount of the subsidy for charitable contributions is approximately three cents. This doesn't sound like much but what if I told you that the total amount of the government subsidy given to individuals over the past four years, for their charitable contributions, was $204 billion?
- If you have an Individual Retirement Account (IRA), you don't have to pay income taxes on the money you put into it. Nor do you have to pay taxes on the accumulating interest or capital gains. This subsidy cost the federal government $722 billion over the past four years.
- What if you are really frugal and purchase tax-exempt municipal bonds? Fine, but the rest of us have to subsidize you and your fellow bond holders to the tune of $1 billion each year.
- Do you have a student loan that qualifies for special tax status? Somebody must because the cost to subsidize them was almost $4 billion over the past four years.
- Do you have kids at home under the age of 17? Apparently a lot of folks must, because the government has given $68 billion in tax credits (subsidies) over the past four years to those households that do.
- Did you insulate your home over the past four years? Good for you. I'm sure you saved a bundle on your

energy bill, but please tell me why the government had to subsidize you and the rest of your friends and neighbors who did the same, to the tune of $2 billion?

- Did you sell your house in the past four years? I know the market has been really tough for those of you who did, but one piece of good news is that you didn't have to pay capital gains on your profit. Why not? I don't know. But I do know that the subsidy given to you and your countrymen who did likewise was $90 billion.

- Are you an avid supporter of your favorite University? Personally, I'm a Spartan (go Michigan State!), but my brother is a Wolverine (boo, University of Michigan). But both of us can deduct our contributions to these schools. Why? Not sure, but the government was willing to subsidize our gifts to the tune of $40 billion over the last four years. No, not just me and my brother— everyone.

And the list goes on and on and on.

So now that we have had a look at the subsidies given by the government to average folks like you and me, we can really get mad when we look at what the "big corporations" and "fat cats" got over the past four years.

• Research and development	$40 billion
• Wind power	$4 billion
• Clean-coal technologies	$800 million
• Oil and gas exploration	$7 billion
• Building low-income housing	$30 billion
• Historic Restoration	$2 billion
• Accelerated Depreciation	$9 billion

And the list goes on and on and on.

Why does this happen? Conservatives believe that politicians of every stripe just can't help themselves. They complain about soaring government debt, but any time they can give a subsidy to a constituent in order to win their vote (average Joe's like you and me), or a "big corporation" or "fat cat" to get a campaign contribution, they will do so without a moment's hesitation. This has to stop. And the only way to stop it is to eliminate any and all subsidies for everyone. Conservatives believe that the marketplace is where the value of a good or service should be determined, and the market should be free to do so without the influence of trillions of dollars in government subsidies to millions of people and corporations.

By the way, we might want to go a bit easier on the "big corporations" and "fat cats" who are feeding at the public trough. They receive about $300 billion of subsidies each year, while the subsidies to individuals like you and me total over $1 trillion per year. Yep, that's right. The average Joe's get more than the corporations do. Now, if you combine the subsidies that Washington gives to individuals and corporations every year, it comes to $1.3 trillion. Now, why does that number ring a bell? Oh yeah, that's the same amount as our federal budget deficit every year. Isn't that amazing? Politicians scream about the deficit, but it's caused by them giving subsidies to every Tom, Dick, and Harry in the country, plus the companies they work for. If you would like to see a detailed breakdown of all of these subsidies, go to the web page of the Joint Committee on Taxation published by the U.S. Congress; you can read the 80-page document for yourself.

Chapter 12

The Separation of Church and State

Conservatives understand that nowhere in the Constitution does it say the words "separation of church and state," but they also believe that since we live in a pluralistic society, it's probably a good idea.

The confusion regarding the separation of church and state is simple. These two institutions have separate functions in our society, but the participants in both overlap to a great degree. When they do overlap, one has to take precedence over the other. Conservatives believe that when a person is under the domain of the church, they are free to act out their religious preferences in any manner that the church deems appropriate. When, however, they are under the domain of the state, their religious freedoms are subject to some limitations.

Put plainly, if you are at church, you can restrict the gathering to people who believe like you and you can all sing, dance, clap, pray, preach, and worship to your heart's content. But if you want to practice your religion on the steps of the courthouse, you have to either share the stage with non-believers or agree with them that perhaps both of you could find a more appropriate venue, avoiding the conflict altogether. What conservatives don't believe is that one religion (including atheism) should be allowed to occupy the city square at the exclusion of all others.

If you care to, you can read the Constitutional arguments, the founding fathers' original intentions, the early debates, and the winding path of court decisions that have brought us to where we are today. This path will lead you past such milestones as Thomas Jefferson's letter to the Baptists at Danbury Connecticut: telling them there should be a wall of separation between church and state. You will see where James Madison wrote a similar letter to a group of Baptists where he stated that a "practical distinction between Religion and Civil Government is essential to the purity of both." And you will meet the "Establishment Clause," where the Constitution states, "Congress shall make no law respecting the establishment of religion." From these starting points, you can witness 200 years of court cases, dissecting this issue a hundred different ways. Or you can deal with it the way conservatives believe it should be dealt with: by respecting others and acting in such a way as to merit respect.

Conservatives deal with the facts as they are, and not as we would like them to be. The fact is that in today's United States there is such a wide disparity of religious beliefs, that even within denominations there is disagreement as to what they stand for. To claim that the United States is a "Christian nation" is to ignore reality and harbors on delusion. Yes, there are millions of Christians in these United States. But this country is a republic, set up under the rule of law, and the law that we are most proud of says that all of us are equal. What do conservatives believe this means? It means that we treat others with respect and in a spirit of humility; we should voluntarily restrict our rights to shout out religious convictions in a public square, even if we have the law on our side.

There are actually very few instances where religious beliefs are in conflict with public policy. Nativity scenes on the lawn of the courthouse, posting the Ten Commandments in courtrooms, and prayer at public school events are a few of the higher profile cases. In the rare event when a group is so adamant about their right to practice their religious beliefs in public and demand that they have this right because of the First Amendment (that's the free-speech amendment), the outcome is that their self-righteous portrayal far outstrips any meaningful message they may have.

Who among us would not give a month's wages to punch the leader of the Westboro Baptist Church in the nose? Conservatives everywhere are sickened with this group's message of hate and damnation on everyone who doesn't agree with them. Yet as vile as this group is, when the courts upheld their right to free speech (restricted, yes, but not denied), we all felt a bit of relief. Someday, another group with an honorable purpose and a legitimate goal of fostering positive change will be allowed to protest. Perhaps even a group you are part of.

Yes, there should be a separation between what I can do and say in the privacy of my home, private school, church, or business, and what I'm allowed to say when the taxpayers are providing the venue. But laws and rules won't solve this problem. Mutual respect and humility is called for first, and conservatives believe that both of these attributes are at the heart of what it means to be conservative. And that is why we also believe that, out of respect for all religions, we should not ask the state to become a decider; rather, as a Jewish rabbi once said, "We should try to live peaceably with all men."

Chapter 13

Property Tax Exemptions for Religious Groups

Conservatives believe that subsidies are wrong, and it doesn't matter if it is intended to encourage people to buy an electric car, or to exempt a group of people from paying property tax because they are worshipping God.

Every Sunday, millions of people gather together to participate in corporate worship. Some of them worship race car drivers who challenge each other on the NASCAR, Formula One, or Indy Car Circuits. Some prefer to worship at the altar of Hollywood greats such as George Clooney, Tom Hanks, and Angelina Jolie as they gather in movie theaters to catch the latest film. Still others set aside their Sundays for the worship of God. All three of these groups have something in common—a shared zeal for something bigger than themselves—and all three entities of this worship require police and fire protection, public roads, sidewalks, street lighting, and utility infrastructure. But only two have to pay for these services.

Conservatives have long argued that singling one group of people out and giving them special treatment not available to others is a poor proposition at best. When this happens, it becomes someone's job to decide who gets the "goodie" and who doesn't. In this case, it will be a bureaucrat or judge making the decision. Unfortunately the tax exemption laws are nebulous enough to turn this into a subjective matter versus an objective one.

Conservatives recognize that even though they believe in limited government, they do believe that there are certain legitimate minimum functions that a municipality must provide its citizens. This includes items on the aforementioned list, and these things cost money. Exempting religious institutions from paying their fair share of property taxes requires everyone else to pay more. When a fire breaks out at the temple, synagogue, church, or mosque, the parishioners would stand shocked in horror if the local fire department just stood by and watched it burn. If a break-in occurred at a church and the police refused to show up to investigate, the local pastor would be very upset. If a gunman walked into a temple and threatened to shoot people, and the cops didn't respond to hysterical 911 calls, the whole community would be livid. If these institutions wish to enjoy the benefits of local and state government when it comes to meeting their physical and safety needs, then they should be obligated to pay their fair share of the cost.

A second reason conservatives believe that religious groups should pay property taxes is that it strengthens their position when they argue the merits about the separation of church and state. This debate about their religious rights could remain focused solely on that, without being clouded by the fact that they are taking advantage of the system when it comes to the physical issues such as police and fire protection. Imagine, if you will, a local church wanting to use the front lawn of the public park to erect a Nativity scene or a local church group wanting to sing in a public place, such as on the courthouse steps. The fact that they are a taxpaying entity gives them "standing," if you will. The logic of the argument would be: we pay taxes and we should be able to use the facilities just like anyone else. Demands such as this, while asking society as a whole to foot the bill for the venue, are a bit disingenuous.

Third, leaving aside the cops and firefighters for a moment, let's think about the problems that now arise when a church wishes to buy a piece of farm land, commercial property, or industrial parcel in order to build a new worship facility on it. Don't think for a moment that the local officials are very thrilled about losing the property tax revenue due to this new building. Our construction company builds a lot of churches and we have seen this first-hand. Communities don't mind if a church builds in their area, they just don't like the fact that they are now out the revenue they were counting on.

Fourth, and this is where the problem really gets weird: how far into the private economy can the religious institution go without violating the privilege of not paying property taxes? Can they have a child-care or retirement facility on campus without paying taxes? Can they have a for-profit school use part of the church building and not pay taxes? Can they offer recreational facilities such as workout rooms, cafes, bookstores health clinics or banquet halls, all without paying taxes? Kind of dicey, isn't it? Because all of these functions would have competitors in the free market who would love to be able to operate property tax-free.

Finally, it has been argued that requiring a religious institution to pay its share of local property taxes would allow local politicians to drive some of them out of "business" because they could maliciously raise their taxes so high that the group simply couldn't afford them—but that is not true. Local politicians don't control the assessed value of any properties in their communities; that is what assessors do. Once an assessor determines the value of a given piece of property, his or her findings can be challenged at a review board. Here, taxpayers (either individuals, business owners, or in this case, the religious group), can argue against the assessment in a public forum using appropriate data such as comparable property values or replacement cost estimates. Once the value has been settled, all of the properties of the same classification (residential, industrial, commercial) pay the same rate, usually a percentage of their value in property taxes.

Conservatives believe that all people, and by extension the organizations to which they belong, should be treated equally. Giving some a tax break based on subjective criteria is rife with conflict and full of opportunity to take advantage of the system. This would not exist with the elimination of the property tax-exempt status of religious institutions.

By the way, this argument extends to nonprofit organizations as well.

Chapter 14

Socialism

To say that conservatives believe that socialism is wrong is too simplistic. Because the word itself is used very loosely by any number of pundits, it is important to define what it really is, and then provide the correct conservative response. The response for the purposes of this book is the one where conservatives define liberal behavior as "socialistic." This word seems to be a favorite description of the left from many in the conservative camp, but what does it really mean, and are we correct in our assessment of them?

When someone is called a socialist, it means that they want the government involved in people's lives a little bit (or in some cases a lot) more than the person leveling the accusation. However, let's be honest, we all benefit from communal ownership of some sort or another. For instance, I fly my own airplane. If it weren't for the government providing funding for the construction of small airports around the country, I would not have anywhere to take-off or land. Not being able to build my own airports, I use theirs instead. Does that make me a socialist? No. Similarly, when we, as citizens, pool our resources (taxes) and decide as a group that we want to use those funds to build roads, bridges, schools, or fire stations, this does not make us all socialists.

A socialist is someone who prefers to take money from the general population in the form of taxes and redistribute these funds in areas of the economy where the private sector is supposed to operate. In doing so, the private sector is harmed (and many times driven out of business), leaving the government as the sole provider of this good or service.

The following examples would qualify:

- If a person feels that it is the government's duty and responsibility to provide public education to the exclusion of charter, private, or parochial options, then they just might be a socialist.
- If a person believes that it is the government's duty and responsibility to provide healthcare to the exclusion of private hospitals, doctors, and clinics using private insurance or cash, they just might be a socialist.
- If a person believes that it is the government's duty to subsidize some industries (such as renewable energy) at the expense of others such as oil, gas, or coal, they just might be a socialist.
- If a person believes that the government has the right (through the process called eminent domain) to forcibly buy private property from one private individual, only to sell it to another private individual who will develop it in a manner that a government official approves of, they just might be a socialist.
- If a person believes that the government has a duty and a right to force private banks to buy insurance from them (think FDIC) so that they, the government, would be the sole source of remedy in the event of a collapse, they just might be a socialist.
- If a person believes that it is the duty and the right of the government to tell all private business owners, regardless of the size or type of business they own, the minimum amount they must pay all of their employees, they just might be a socialist.

- If a person believes that it is the duty of the government to impose tariffs on imported goods so that all Americans have to pay more for those goods to the benefit of a few jobs saved, they just might be a socialist.
- If a person feels that the taxes levied on successful business owners, risk takers, and entrepreneurs should be steadily raised as their income from success rises, and the resulting tax revenue "spread around" to the rest of society, they just might be a socialist.

Calling someone a socialist just because they are liberal is not an accurate assessment. There are many liberal positions where there is simply no basis for this type of accusation. However, when a person feels that it is the government's duty to step in and disrupt the private economy in ways similar to those outlined above, the label is quite accurate.

Chapter 15

Capitalism and Greed

Conservatives are unrepentantly strong believers that capitalism is, by far and away, the best method to bring prosperity to the largest amount of people in the most efficient and economical way possible.

Conservatives believe that the only way to create wealth is through commerce. Period. Conservatives know and understand that simply printing money and spreading it around does not work—southern Europe is a prime example of what happens to an economy when this happens. Conservatives also understand that while borrowing money to buy capital goods is prudent in some cases, the act of borrowing alone does not create wealth. For instance; if I have $100 and borrow another $100, I'm not suddenly worth $200. I'm still only "worth" $100. However, if I take my $200 and invest it in a stock which doubles in value, then my $200 becomes $400. I can then pay back my loan of $100 and I am now "worth" $300—not because I borrowed the money, but because I bought and sold something. That, in a nutshell, is called capitalism.

Recently capitalism has come under tremendous criticism from many different directions. It has been demonized as a system that preys on the poor and unfortunate, and is also blamed for many (if not all) of our social ills and financial failures. The truth is exactly the opposite. The reason people believe this is because they don't understand what the basis of true capitalism is. The basic fundamental principle of capitalism is greed. And the definition of greed is *an excessive desire for more of something than is needed.*

Capitalism is based upon people in society always wanting more, and never being totally content with their situation, whatever it may be. Because of this, each person works to improve his or her lot in life. This process of improving involves many things such as gaining an education, working hard, taking risks, and constantly looking for ways to better their lives. When each person in society does this, the society as a whole improves and life, in general, gets better for everyone. The contrast to capitalism is socialism where, as pointed out in the previous chapter, the focus is not on individual efforts but government intervention. To use the examples of the last chapter:

- If you believe that the public school in your area is underperforming and that the parents of the kids who go there would pay you a profit to teach their kids in a private school that you are considering opening, you just might be a capitalist. If you open this school because you feel that the profit you might make from it will make you happier, you are definitely a capitalist.
- If you believe that by getting a medical degree you can take advantage of the fact that the marketplace will pay you handsomely for your services, you just might be a capitalist. If you do get a degree, open a clinic and make a handsome profit, which makes you happier, you are definitely a capitalist.
- If you believe that you know where there is oil in the ground and that if you dig a well and find it, you could make a bunch of money, you just might be a capitalist. If you actually do spend all of your money on this

dream, but in the end go broke trying, only to try again, you are definitely a capitalist.

- If you see an underutilized piece of property that, if purchased at the right price from the owner, could be turned into a profitable enterprise, you just might be a capitalist. If you do reach an agreement to buy the property, develop it and make money enjoying the fruits of your labor, you are definitely a capitalist.

- If you observe that people are leery of putting their money in a bank that might go broke, resulting in a total loss of their funds, and you formulate a way through private insurance to mitigate this risk for them, you just might be a capitalist. If you invest all your time, energy, and money to start an insurance company that provides this insurance, and enjoy the profits you make from this business, you are definitely a capitalist.

- If you have an idea for a small business and know that you could get the teenagers in your neighborhood to work for you at a wage which would allow you to make a profit, you just might be a capitalist. If you actually do start a business, and hire these kids for a low wage— providing them with entry-level jobs and you with a nice profit to enjoy —you are definitely a capitalist.

- If you are considering opening a business whose product is easily importable from a number of countries that have wages considerably lower than yours, you just might be a capitalist. If you open this business, knowing the risks involved, and ultimately go broke because you just can't compete with the imports, you are definitely a capitalist.

- If you believe that through hard work, skill, and risk-taking the money you might make should not be taxed at a higher rate than what it would have been if you didn't succeed, then you just might be a capitalist. If, knowing that you will be punished for your success, you still push on in the face of adversity and ultimately succeed, you are definitely a capitalist.

Now, getting back to the definition of greed and why it is the fundamental principle of capitalism. Greed involves wanting more than *"is needed."* This is a very important aspect of capitalism. If everyone in society was content with what they had, and no one wanted more than what they simply needed to get by, then the capitalist system would not work as well. No one would buy or trade any more than what was necessary, and so companies would not hire any more workers than absolutely necessary. No one would take advantage of opportunities in the marketplace, so no profits would be generated and no wealth would be created. No one would improve their skills to advance their plight, and the whole society would be less educated and poorer for it. When people want more than what is needed—or to put it another way, are greedy—good things happen. If they are really greedy, then great things happen.

Why, then, is "greedy" a bad word? Because when people think of the word "greedy," they usually think of what people do with their wealth once they get it, not the principle that allowed them to accumulate it in the first place. Think of the rich miser, sitting in his mansion with billions of dollars in the bank, while the opportunity to use that money for good is setting idle. Yes, that person is greedy and no, conservatives would not agree with his actions. To understand conservatism, one must understand capitalism, and all conservatives are capitalists.

Chapter 16

Israel

Israel's Prime Minister, Benjamin Netanyahu, recently remarked that if the countries surrounding Israel put down their weapons, there would be peace in a day. If Israel put down its weapons, they (Israel) would be wiped out overnight. This backdrop is important as we look at a conservative's belief that Israel is special, and merits unique consideration.

Support for Israel is not necessarily due to the common heritage that many Christian conservatives share with Israel. Yes, the first 39 books of the Christian Bible are inherently Jewish Scripture. And yes, dozens of ancient Jewish people are the focus of the stories that Christian parents tell their children. However, there are many conservatives who are not Christian who support Israel, and there are many Christians who are not conservatives who don't. So, why do conservatives support Israel?

First, because conservatives support democracy and Israel is a democracy. In a land that is dominated by theocrats, dictators, monarchs, and families of despots; Israel's leaders are freely elected by its people and provide a beacon of hope in an area of the world filled with dysfunctional and autocratic governments.

Second, because Israel has chosen to be our friend. That's right, this is a two-way street. Simply by a process of elimination, we should support Israel because the vast majority of the governments in the Middle East hate the United States, or at best are very suspicious or leery of us. This is not the case with

Israel. Israel makes no apologies for the fact that they seek the approval and advice of the United States in almost everything they do in the realm of national security. They ask our opinion, and they value our counsel. Contrast this with almost every other nation in the region, with the possible exception of Turkey and Jordan.

Third, it's in the United States' best interest to do so. Israel is strong militarily, economically, and socially. The business community is growing due to the large number of entrepreneurs and risk takers who combine hard work and knowledge to develop an economy that is diverse and stable. United States businesses gain economically by trading with Israeli businesses, and this is good for both countries. Again, compare this with any other country in the region and it's very clear that the U.S. should support Israel out of national self-interest.

Fourth, Israel has a first-rate intelligence community and we need intelligence in this part of the world in a very bad way. The Middle East is a powder keg with the confluence of wealthy, oil-rich nations subverting human rights; poor countries rattling sabers to divert attention from their own economic plight; dictators killing thousands of their own people; and Islamist extremists in power in some of the largest nations. With all of this strife, hatred, war, and upheaval in a very important area of the globe, we must rely on first-rate intelligence to navigate clearly, and Israel provides it. It's important to note that one of Israel's enemies has publicly vowed to "wipe it off the map." With this kind of rhetoric flying around and getting traction in several world capitals, it's easy to see that the stakes are high and we need to know what is going on there at all times.

Finally, our support of Israel is necessary to counter-balance the influence of Russia in the region. If we were to remove our strong and unequivocal support for Israel, Russia and its allies in Iran and Syria would have a green-light to cause mischief beyond belief. Since the fall of the Soviet Union, Russia has seen its influence wane in many areas of the world, including the Caribbean, where it supported the Castro regime; Eastern Europe, where dozens of former communist bloc countries were under its control; and China, where trade with the U.S. has given us a much stronger position of influence with the Chinese. The last thing Russia wants is to lose what little control they have left in the Middle East. Evidence of their support for Syria and Iran are proof of this. These two countries hate Israel, and Russia's power, wealth, and influence would go unchecked in the region if the United States didn't strongly defend and support Israel.

Conservatives believe that Israel is a strong ally and we should support them in the same unashamed and brazen way we do all of our allies, worldwide. If we vacillate in our support for just a moment, the results could be disastrous.

Chapter 17

Guns

The Second Amendment to the Constitution makes the right to own a gun the law of the land. The Supreme Court has ruled that it applies to civilians and not just militia, and it has also ruled that local and state governments can't overrule this right. I won't bore you with a 900-word defense of something that doesn't need to be defended. The case for the right of Americans to possess a firearm is closed.

But conservatives don't believe that just because something is legal, it is right. Conservatives truly do believe that gun ownership is a good thing, whether or not it is a right granted under the Constitution. Because of this we hope that the logic of our argument will convince skeptics that they should reconsider their position on the subject.

First, conservatives understand that our opponents want to take away our right to own a gun because they genuinely feel that gun ownership is a problem. Our job is to show them that it is not. If we can solve the systemic issue (and I think we can), then the argument will be over.

Let's start with a fact.

Many people are killed each day and the weapon of choice is a gun.

Here's another fact. Conservatives are just as disgusted by this as everyone else.

I live in Michigan, and some parts of this state are as pristine as any place in the world. However, the cities of Detroit, Flint, and Saginaw are as notorious for their violence today as they were for building great cars in years past. I grew up about 30 miles from Saginaw. I saw how this city fell into decay and neglect when the auto companies pulled out and the jobs went with them. Forty-five years ago, crime was a factor, but shootings were rare. Bay City, a town of 50,000 where I was born, would go all year without a murder. Gun laws? No one talked about them because no one was being killed by them. This was the case in much of the United States in the middle part of the last century. In high school, I would debate with my more liberal friends about the morality of hunting (protecting animals versus harvesting them for food, etc…) but never did they suggest that I didn't have a right to own a gun. Things have changed over the past 40 years. As the fabric of our society has started to unravel, traditional sources and practices of social structure including solid families, church attendance, union hall meetings, and safe urban public schools went by the wayside. Replacing these institutions was a whole new way of social gathering. Movie theaters with incredibly violent shows became our churches. Court rulings limiting the ability of school administrators to deliver discipline changed our public schools from safe havens to hazard zones. Divorce and the acceptance of "living together" made traditional families consisting of one mom and one dad look downright old fashioned and un-hip. Union halls where men and women of like mind gathered to pledge their unity to one another were abandoned or reduced in size reflecting the precipitous drop in membership.

The tide turning against traditional values and civility in general seemed to turn in the early 1960s. Drug use and the hippie movement, which encouraged people to "tune in, turn on, and drop out," resulted in a general lack of personal responsibility on the part of young people everywhere. By the late sixties, Detroit was burning and the wholesale destruction in parts of this once mighty city was well underway. Looking back it seems unthinkable that the National Guard had to be called out just to restore calm in the streets.

I could go on and on, but even the most casual observer would have to admit that society has changed over the past couple of generations and not necessarily for the better. We are living in a much more violent and, dare I say, evil time then just a few decades ago.

Now how does this relate to gun ownership and the conservative's belief that it is necessary and proper?

First, it's for personal protection in a violent place. Simply stated, I believe that owning a gun will provide protection to me and my family when someone tries to cause us harm. No, conservatives do not believe that we have the right to shoot someone if we merely feel threatened by them, as some have suggested. Conservatives are opposed to laws that would give a shooter the right to be judge, jury, and executioner. But it has come to the point in society where law-abiding people feel threatened when going to the store, a movie theater, or church because we look around and see that shootings by crazy people are not theoretical anymore, they are real.

Second, if you live in an area with high gun violence, the chances are that the people shooting each other have nothing to do with you, but are "settling scores" of past shootings, drug deals that have gone bad, or simple gang violence. However, thousands of people have found themselves in the middle of these situations with no means of protection at all. If that is how you want to be found, fine—just don't ask me to unilaterally lay down my right to protect myself while the outlaws have a field day.

Third, the bad guys are getting bolder. Recently in our area, an elderly couple was the target of a gang of hoodlums who would walk by their home on a daily basis and threaten them with taunts and warnings such as, "One of these days we're gonna rob you guys." The old couple tried to complain to the police, but reports of predicted violence don't get noticed down at the police station when they are dealing with real violence on a daily basis. Sure enough, one day while the couple was inside their home, the front door was kicked in. Striding through the opening was the same thug who had been shouting the threats the day before. Boldly he headed straight for the older couple with a gang of fellow thugs close behind. All of a sudden, the old man pulled a shotgun out from under the couch and blew the idiot away. The rest of the gang scattered. The great equalizer had emerged. This couple cannot "flee to the suburbs" like many have done. They own their home in the city of Detroit and couldn't sell it if they had to. They are imprisoned there for the rest of their lives. Unfortunately, owning a gun is not a luxury for them, it's a survival weapon.

My guess is that most liberals who oppose gun ownership live in areas where they don't need them to survive. Perhaps you live in one of those areas. Good for you. But I don't. Let's you and me take a ride down Grand Boulevard someday. You will have the car doors locked, windows up, and will ask me not to stop for a red light. You will also be glad I can defend you if I have to.

Chapter 18

Buy American?

There's a reason Derek Jeter doesn't mow his own lawn. It's not that he isn't strong enough. It's not that he doesn't want to, and it's certainly not because he can't afford a lawn mower. The reason Derek Jeter doesn't mow his own lawn is because he makes one million dollars a month (after taxes) as the shortstop for the New York Yankees. Taking one day off to mow his lawn would cost him about $30,000 in lost wages, even though he could do it for less than $5.00 in gas. Derek Jeter has what is called a "comparative advantage" over everyone else when it comes to playing shortstop for the Yankees. When his time is concentrated on this effort, his income is maximized and his wealth grows the fastest. There is no doubt that Derek Jeter could do something else other than play baseball. He would probably be a good brick layer. He would probably be able to do a lot of jobs that required manual labor such as carpentry, welding, steel erection, or painting. But if the truth were told, he would probably not do these other jobs quite as well as the people who have a comparative advantage over him in those fields. He might be good, but someone who is better would be able to do the job faster and more efficiently than Derek Jeter, and he would struggle to make even a small fraction of what he makes playing shortstop. So, even though he could do any of these other jobs, if he's not the best he won't be able to be competitive with the other guys and it just wouldn't make sense for him to try.

Now let's pretend for a moment that we have a whole country of "Derek Jeters." Let's call this country the United States. In the same manner as Derek Jeter, the United States does some things really well and some things not as well as others. For instance, the United States designs and markets the greatest computers and cell phones in the world. We have a comparative advantage in that area over every other country on the planet. However, we don't make them here, because some other country that is more efficient at making small electronic devices than we are enjoys a comparative advantage in that area. Now let's pause here for a second and examine what would happen if, for some reason, everyone in the United States was forced to buy computers or cell phones that were not only designed and marketed here, but also produced here. Well, this would be like the New York Yankees insisting that Derek Jeter not only play shortstop, but sell hot dogs between innings as well. Instead of paying a local kid the government-mandated minimum wage of $7.25, the Yankees would have Jeter do it. Now Jeter is a smart guy and he knows he can play shortstop for many other teams if he needs to. So, even though he agrees to sell hot dogs, he does so upon one condition: that his salary stays at $30,000 per day, or what amounts to about $4,000 per hour. "No problem," the Yankees say, "We'll just change the price of the hot dogs accordingly, so that we at least break even." And so that's what they do. Subsequently we find out that Jeter is pretty good at selling hot dogs as well. But not good enough to cover his salary without everyone in the stadium having to pay a little bit more for the fact that the Yankees are serving these hot dogs with their own players, rather than going outside the organization and hiring it done a lot cheaper. In the end, the price of a hot dog goes from $5.00 to $15.00 (Jeter sold 400 in just one hour and because the difference between the old price and new is

77

$10.00 he at least covered his salary). Adding $10.00 per hot dog doesn't sound like that big of a deal. However, consider two things. The average person who bought that hot dog is now out about an hours' worth of wages, and the whole group that bought the hot dogs are $4,000 poorer than what they would have been, had the local kid made the sale. After the sales of hot dogs plummet, the Yankees decide to go back to hiring the kid from the outside to sell the hot dogs, and let Jeter do what he does best: play shortstop. This is exactly what would happen if, for some reason, say, a bunch of politicians decided to whip up some nationalistic sentiment and cry, "We should only buy computers and cell phones that are made in America." So, instead of buying from countries that offered a comparative advantage for these items, we restricted our choices to American firms only. The problem is the same one the Yankees had when they tried to use their players to sell hot dogs. Oh, it can be done alright, but you aren't going to like the hit that you take to your pocketbook. In some cases, as in computers and cell phones, you may find that the price is more than doubled.

There is another problem with "Buy American" programs and I experienced it firsthand. Our company does business throughout North America; this includes Canada, Mexico, and the Caribbean. A couple of years ago, we were on the cusp of getting a very large contract with a company that will remain nameless in Montreal. I traveled to this beautiful Canadian city six times to present our proposal and tried to convince them that the Wieland-Davco Corporation would be their best choice of general contractors. One day, during negotiations, the president of the United States went on a "Buy American" crusade to gain political points at a union rally. My counterpart at the Canadian company called me up and said this: "Craig, how are we going to justify hiring an American company like yours when your president is urging our customers in the United States to drop us in favor of our American competitor?" My heart sank. All my hard work was about to be lost along with the American jobs that would have resulted in this contract.

A third problem with "Buy American" is that many times the only way to accomplish this goal is either to raise the cost of incoming goods to the United States (through tariffs) to make them as expensive as the American ones or to subsidize American companies so that they can compete in the global marketplace. While these may sound like good ideas at first, as with most government solutions to perceived problems in the marketplace, the unintended consequence of this usually is that the opposing country retaliates in some fashion and a trade war thus ensues. In a trade war, nobody ever wins; there are only greater and lesser degrees of losers.

Conservatives understand that we live in a global economy, and as such we need to make decisions that allow the United States, as a whole, to prosper as much as we can. Urging (or in some cases requiring) American consumers or businesses to "Buy American" may make a great slogan for a bumper sticker, but it stinks from an economic standpoint. American companies are the best in the world and when allowed to compete in the free market, they usually come out on top. Every now and then, there are areas where other countries have a comparative advantage over the U.S. In those cases we should take advantage of the situation and buy their goods.

I, for one, don't want to pay more just to be eating hot dogs sold by Derek Jeter.

Chapter 19

Buy Local!

If you, the reader, have already read the conservative position on "Buy American," you have probably already jumped to the conclusion that conservatives believe that "Buy Local" is wrong as well—all that "comparative advantage" stuff considering. Well, you'd be wrong.

As stated elsewhere in this book, conservatives make principled decisions. But, as stated elsewhere as well, all principles are not of equal importance. And "Buy Local" is a prime example of one principle taking precedence over another.

First, the "lower" principle. Conservatives believe in the efficiency of the free market system. We believe that we should always buy the product that represents the best combination of quality, price, and availability, regardless of its origin. If your product isn't competitive on the basis of these three objective criteria, then sorry, we will buy from the one that is.

Now, the "higher" principle. Conservatives believe that it is the responsibility of the local community, starting with family, then with friends, and finally extending to the neighborhood, to address the needs of those who are looking for a helping hand or needing a bit of a boost. Conservatives are opposed to governmental solutions that emanate from the state, and even more strongly opposed when solutions arrive from Washington. No, conservatives believe that if your neighbor is in need of food, shelter, clothing, transportation, or a little bit of cash to get them through a rough patch, that we should help them out ourselves, and not send them to, in my case, Lansing, or worse, Washington D.C. And this is why "Buy Local" is important.

Most of us who have jobs get up every morning, drink our coffee, and head to work. If we stop anywhere we get gas at a local station, but don't go inside because we now have "pay at the pump." Once at work, and due to our global economy, we talk to people all over the world. Just before 5:00pm, we log onto the internet and buy books, clothes, golf shoes, chain saws, bullets, you name it; and then head home. Snug in our dens, we watch TV and then after a while retire to bed, only to repeat the same ritual all over again the next day.

A Jewish rabbi once gave a command that is universally accepted as a good mantra to live by: "Love your neighbor as yourself." Conservatives think this is a good idea, but question how we can love our neighbors if we don't even know them? That's where "Buy Local" comes in. Conservatives believe that the higher principle to help those in need can only be accomplished by knowing those in need. This knowledge is obtained by going to local restaurants (in lieu of mail-order steaks from 2,000 miles away) and actually getting to know the waitress. By visiting the local farmers market, not because you think you can buy food with the highest possible quality at the lowest possible price like you probably could from the giant superstore at the edge of town; it's because you want to get to know the people who grow the food, and hear their stories of joys and sorrows. Buy your suits from the local haberdasher, who could tell you about his grandfather starting the business, and who will appreciate your patronage more than you can imagine. Finally, go to your locally-owned hardware store. Get to know the owners and employees there by their first names, and then someday, one of them will say to you, *"Hey, Joe, I got this problem and I need a little help."* It will be music to your ears, because that same Jewish rabbi also said, "It's better to give than to receive."

Conservatives believe that helping their neighbors is their responsibility first and the government's second; and buying local is one way they stay in touch with their neighbors. This way they know them well enough in the good times that they can be there for them in the bad.

Chapter 20

Defending Big Salaries

"There's no way that guy (in this case a shortstop) is worth $20 million," a friend of mine (who calls himself a conservative, by the way) stated emphatically. "Really?" I asked. "Let me ask you a question. What do you think your boss would pay you if you could get 40,000 people to show up at your cubicle every day, just to watch you work?" He grinned—knowing that he couldn't get four people to do that. "Yeah, I never thought about it that way. I guess if his boss thinks he's worth it, then to him, perhaps he is," he said.

Conservatives believe that, over time, everyone is paid exactly what he or she is worth to society. I know if you are a teacher and get paid 1/100 of what an average Major League shortstop gets, you think something is wrong. Well, there is nothing necessarily wrong with the way we compensate different jobs at different amounts; it's just that society values shortstops more than teachers.

In a capitalistic society people are free to spend their disposable income however they want. When they do spend it, they want the maximum value for the minimum investment. If you look around our society, you will see plenty of areas where many people would say that money is not being spent wisely. This might include venues such as sports stadiums, movie theaters, casinos, nightclubs, and fancy restaurants. But if that is where consumers find value, then that is where they are going to spend their money, and the people who work in or run these establishments will make big salaries.

Big salaries are nothing new. The robber barons of the 19th century made millions of dollars in basic industries such as oil, railroads, steel, and lumber. But what allowed them to make such huge sums? The product they made brought value to millions of people's lives. The people needed oil, steel, and lumber to build and heat their homes. They needed the railroad to transport their goods and go on vacations. In modern times, Bill Gates and Steve Jobs became multi-billionaires by bringing tremendous value to billions of people's lives, through their high-tech products. Meanwhile, our teachers toil long hours, at very difficult jobs, for what they believe is meager pay. Consumers of their product (taxpayers and/or parents if the school is private) have yet to understand their value. If teachers can raise the perceived value of their services, their pay will go up. If they can't, then it won't.

A classic example of this is when, in 1930, Babe Ruth was criticized for making more money than President Hoover. When asked to defend his salary, Ruth simply stated, "I had a better year than the president." In fact, what he meant was that the people in the United States in 1930 valued the service that he provided more than they valued the service that the president provided.

Recently, a group of people have been singled out as egregious offenders in this area. These are the so-called "fat cats" that work in the financial sector of our economy, or what is otherwise known as Wall Street. It appears that these people make way more money than the average person believes they are worth. But these people all have bosses who, without coercion, have agreed to the terms of their employment. In the "dog-eat-dog" world of Wall Street, if anyone thinks they can make a buck by paying less money in salaries to their employees, they most certainly will. So why don't they? Because they value the services that these people provide so much that they are willing to pay them millions of dollars per year to do it. Just like the shortstop. But what about the top guys at these firms? Don't they have bosses? Yes they do. A properly-functioning board of directors will see to it that each "top guy" gets paid in accordance with the value they are bringing to the firm. (See Chapter 54 Corporate Oversight).

Let's be honest. We would all love to have a job that pays $20 million per year. But the vast majority of us simply do not bring that kind of value to society. We can't hit a 98 mph fastball, turn a double play, structure a business merger, pick stock winners, or simply sing or act better than everybody else. If we could, we would be rich. Very rich.

Conservatives believe that the market should determine salaries and understand that what the market values, it pays for.

Chapter 21

When Life Begins

No issue is more polarizing than abortion. No issue causes more contention and no issue is as divisive as a woman's right to terminate her pregnancy, prior to the baby being born.

The definition of when life begins is the basic element in the abortion argument. Conservatives believe that if a person is "alive," then they have certain rights outlined by the Declaration of Independence, among these being the right to life. Remember: life, liberty, and the pursuit of happiness? If a person (the baby in question) has "life," then it is our duty as a society to protect that life and not terminate it or destroy it without due process of law.

But when does a person/baby/fetus/embryo have life? Conservatives believe the moment the egg is fertilized by the sperm, life begins. Why? Three reasons.

First, a conservative believes that neither sperm nor eggs on their own would be described as "alive" because both lack the ability to produce a human being apart from the other. However, once they come together the probability of a human being exiting the womb in nine months is extremely high. Conservatives believe that once this event (referred to by most as conception) takes place, life has begun, and to stop it should be considered murder.

Second, if not conception, then when? Conservatives believe that if a person is not considered alive at conception then identifying a future milestone when they *would* be is a slippery slope indeed.

In a matter of weeks, the baby will develop a heartbeat, lungs, tiny hands, feet, and will be covered with a thin layer of skin. Is the baby alive yet?

By the end of the baby's second month in the womb, webbed fingers and toes are poking out from their hands and feet, their eyelids practically cover their eyes, breathing tubes extend from their throat to the branches of their developing lungs, In their brain, nerve cells are branching out to connect with one another, forming primitive neural pathways. Is the baby alive yet?

By the end of the third month the baby's fingers will soon begin to open and close and their toes will curl, eye muscles will clench, and their mouth will make sucking movements. In fact, the baby's intestines, which have grown so fast that they protrude into the umbilical cord, will start to move into their abdominal cavity and their kidneys will begin excreting urine into their bladder. Is the baby alive yet?

By month four the baby's heart is pumping 25 quarts of blood each day. Is the baby alive yet?

Month five; the baby is 3/4 of a pound, and small nudges turn into full-fledged kicks! Is the baby alive yet?

Month six; the baby's lungs are forming branches and their skin is starting to gain color. Is the baby alive yet?

Month seven; the baby is blinking her eyes. Is she alive yet?

Month eight; she now has toenails, fingernails, and real hair. Is she alive yet?

Month nine; the baby is beautiful, and she is almost completely out of her mother's womb. Only the lower half of her body is still inside. Is she alive yet? If you answer no to this or any previous question, then by law, you can still kill her.

Finally, conservatives are called "conservative" because the very word speaks about caution and safety. If an issue is gray, such as when life begins, then a conservative will naturally migrate toward the safest assumption, especially when a more lenient view results in a grave consequence, such as death.

Chapter 22

Women's Rights

There is a big difference between how conservatives believe a woman should be treated in society and the rights of a woman in general. This difference is often exploited by liberals who feel that if a woman is treated or expected to act in any way whatsoever different than a man, then somehow, to put it in their language *"conservatives are at war with women."* This could not be further from the truth.

First, conservatives believe that all human beings deserve to be treated with respect and dignity, regardless of their gender. It means that a woman should enjoy all the rights that a man enjoys, with the only exceptions being when it is ridiculous to accommodate the anomaly. For instance, a man doesn't necessarily have the right to serve tables at a topless bar, and a woman doesn't necessarily have a right to play in a men's tennis tournament. These extreme exceptions notwithstanding, conservatives believe that everyone should be judged on their character, skill, ability, male and female alike.

Second, conservatives also believe that women play a special role in our society, and for that reason must be treated differently. For instance, conservative men believe in the old fashioned notion of chivalry and its modern version we call manners. Because of this, a conservative will honor a woman by opening the door for her, insisting that she enter and exit an elevator first, help her with her coat, light her cigarette, drop her off at the door of the restaurant, hold her chair for her when she arrives at the table, and stand when she leaves. Conservative men also believe that it is appropriate to compliment a woman on her appearance, walk slower if the woman is small in stature, and offer to help in any situation, where the woman might need an extra hand. They do this out of respect and honor. They do this because they are gentlemen, not because they feel they need to pander or be overly protective. They do this because they understand that there are profound differences between men and women and by showing deference in the above-mentioned ways, they acknowledge that women are special.

Third, conservatives understand that there are certain principles that are so important that they go beyond a woman's individual rights, and this includes the right to abort her fetus. The conservative believes that life begins at conception, and once life exists it is protected by the Constitution; killing it without due process of law is wrong. Asking a woman to carry a baby to full term and delivering that baby into the outside world is a huge request, but allowing the killing of an innocent human being is not acceptable. Unfortunately, in the case of abortion, there is no middle ground. This would be similar to asking a liberal who is adamantly opposed to capital punishment to somehow accept it as okay. They would reply that taking a life in their mind for any reason is killing, and so therefore will never be okay. Conservatives would say that they feel stronger about their opposition to abortion than liberals feel about capital punishment, simply because no one can argue that the baby in the womb is guilty of any crime whatsoever, but yet must pay the ultimate price by giving up its life.

Finally, conservatives believe a higher principle that would trump a woman's individual rights would be in the area of employment and religious freedom. Stated earlier in this chapter, every woman has a right to be considered for a position in the workplace and should be hired if she is the most qualified person for the job. However, this does not mean that her employer should be required to allow her to exercise her individual rights when they are in conflict with her employer's religious rights. A prime example of this is when a woman works for a religious organization, such as a church. Churches, by their very nature, are organizations whose members share certain religious beliefs which are protected under our Constitution. One such belief is that the use of contraceptives is wrong and should not be used as a means of birth control. This is the official position of the Catholic Church, and one that is espoused by its leaders, from the Pope to the local priest. Catholic churches run Catholic hospitals, and as such employ thousands of people as nurses, doctors, orderlies, receptionists, etc. Many of these employees are women, and many are not Catholic. The recent health care law, passed by Congress and signed by the President, requires all employers to make contraceptives available to employees under the employer's health insurance plan. In other words, women have a right to them. Obviously this includes Catholic hospitals as well. Conservatives believe that women who work for religious organizations do not have the right to demand that the organization violate its own religious beliefs by following the law. Believing that this is an attempt by conservatives to denigrate or "make war" on women is wrong. It's simply an acknowledgement that certain principles are so important that they cannot be impinged upon by a person's individual right, man or woman.

Chapter 23

Roe versus Wade

Just because it's legal, doesn't make it right.

Conservatives believe that the Supreme Court was wrong when it decided in 1973 that:

> *"... the right of privacy, whether it be founded in the Fourteenth Amendment's concept of personal liberty and restrictions upon state action, as we feel it is, or, as the district court determined, in the Ninth Amendment's reservation of rights to the people, is broad enough to encompass a woman's decision whether or not to terminate her pregnancy."*

The decision was 7-2.

Conservatives are pragmatists. We deal with the facts as we find them, not as we wish they were. And the fact is, society has decided that a woman has the right to terminate her pregnancy prior to bringing the baby to term. This issue has been the most polarizing issue in the United States for the past 40 years and will remain its most polarizing issue for the foreseeable future. Because of this, conservatives understand that simply reversing the decision will not solve the problem. Convincing our opponents that our position is the correct one and winning them over to our side with a persuasive argument will save a lot more babies than winning a court case or two.

In the chapter titled "When Life Begins," the conservative position on when a person is alive is very clear. The opposite of having life is *not* having life. That is also called being dead. There are three ways to die. You become ill, in which there is no "fault" to be assigned; you die by accident (again, no "fault" per se); or thirdly—and this is what happens in the case of abortion—you are killed. I know this sounds blunt, but conservatives have a difficult time with nuances.

First, by looking at the debate from a woman's perspective, conservatives understand the argument perfectly. We don't need to be lectured that we just don't understand the plight of a woman who is pregnant and doesn't want to be. I have five daughters and nine grandkids and know full well the difficulties of carrying a child to full term. If you think that because I'm a man I can't possibly understand, then I can point to millions of woman who are just as opposed to abortion as I am who will assure you that they can speak on the issue with first-hand experience.

Second, conservatives agree with the Supreme Court that women have a right to privacy. But women have many rights, and almost all of them are conditional. For instance, a woman has a right to vote, if she has not been convicted of a felony. Society has decided that the right to vote is superseded by a higher principle—the responsibility to behave. Women have the right to free speech, but not to yell "Fire!" in a crowded theater. Women have the right to bear arms, but shooting someone without cause or provocation may bring the revocation of that right. Conservatives believe that a woman's right to privacy is conditional upon her not using this right to kill another living human being.

Third, and this is a big one, conservatives believe that two wrongs don't make a right. As previously mentioned, I have a wife and five daughters. If one of them were ever raped, I would feel compelled to hunt down the offender and kill him with my bare hands. The anger I would feel would be insatiable, and the hate that I would have for this person would know no boundary. If, at the same time, the rape caused a pregnancy, the feelings would rage even more. But I would not consider for a moment that my wife or daughter should kill the baby. Yes, our family would carry the visual image of the rape. We would also be stigmatized by the resulting pregnancy. This situation would wound our pride, cause gossip in the community, and generally ruin our "normal" lives. But killing that baby would be wrong. My daughter or wife might have the right to kill her baby. That right, however unfair as it may seem to her, would be superseded by the baby's right to live.

Fourth, conservatives believe that those who favor the right of a woman to abort her child don't seem to think that they have the responsibility to fully explain the total ramifications, including the mental and emotional stress that this horrible decision is going to cause the woman for the rest of her life. It is clear from the evidence that many young women who have had abortions are traumatized by their decision later on in life. Conservatives observe "pro-choice" advocates ferociously arguing for the right of a woman to have an abortion, but rarely, if ever, have I heard an abortion advocate publicly talking about their concern for a woman's mental stability when she has to confront this decision every day for the rest of her life. I have heard women say they got an abortion and never thought about it again, but conservatives doubt that this is the case. Conservatives believe that women who talk this way are trying to make abortion sound like getting a mole or wart removed. *"I did it and it never bothered me again, so if you are thinking about getting an abortion, don't worry about it. You'll be fine."* Well, millions of women who have had abortions are not fine.

Lastly, conservatives believe that the fight against abortion will be won where the battle is being waged—in the lives of the women who are considering one. My mother has been a tireless worker at Pregnancy Services near the campus of Michigan State University in East Lansing. She has counseled hundreds of young women against getting abortions. In lieu of terminating their pregnancies, Mom and her associates have found adoptive homes for these babies, and many times the pain of the pregnancy has been replaced with the joy of knowing that the little baby will be taken care of. Talk about the difference in that mother's mental well-being, when in the future they can imagine their child being a great scientist, sports hero, business person, or maybe even president.

The abortion battle is the fight for the right of the unborn to simply get a chance to live. If a woman insists that her right to privacy is greater than the right of the baby to live—and we have not done our job as conservatives to convince her otherwise—then we have more work to do. Hoping a bunch of politicians and judges solve this problem for us is wishful thinking, and naive.

Marriage

Conservatives define marriage as the union of one man and one woman.

Liberals define the union of a man to a man or a woman to a woman as same-sex marriage.

It's not the same. The word "marriage" can't be modified by the liberals in the way we might say African-American, as in a subset of Americans. It's been co-opted. It's like Americans wanting to be called Italians. The word marriage, since the beginning of recorded history, has been used to describe the union of one man and one woman.

Conservatives believe that if a man wants to live with a man, in what looks for all intents and purposes like a marriage, and if these two guys want to tell everyone they have a civil union, a mutual understanding, an intimate relationship, are buddies, have a significant other, or even give themselves monikers such as "wife" and "husband," then by all means have at it. The kind of interpersonal relationships a person wants to have with anyone else is their business, and conservatives would argue for their right to do that with our dying breath. Just don't call it marriage, because it's not.

What's the big deal? Why the fuss? The meanings of words change all the time, so why are we so hung up on this one? Because the meaning of a word *can* change if and only if the person using that word agrees to it. What advocates of "same sex" marriage are demanding is that we now include their type of relationships in the description of a word that means something different. If we wanted to, we could. But we don't want to, so we can't be forced to, and we won't.

Some conservatives argue that if we refer to gay unions as "marriage," then we as a society will be forced to extend the social and financial benefits of marriage to their "spouse" as well. But, in the scheme of things that isn't the big deal. Yes, as a conservative, I'm naturally against the expansion of government-provided benefits, but to argue against this word changing on the basis of economics is a ruse. With the government spending $6 billion per day more than it is taking in, I don't see where extending gay live-in partners some added benefits is even germane to the argument. In fact, it's dangerous to even argue that point. This is not an argument about economics. It's an argument about whether people who cannot be married (because they are of the same sex) do so anyway and demand that we change the definition of the word to include their actions.

Why then won't we change the definition of the word? Why are we so hung up on this word that we won't budge? Here's the truth. Because it's sacred. That's right. Sacred.

Conservatives strongly believe in the First Amendment protection of the freedom of religion. Being conservative doesn't necessarily mean we are religious, although a lot of us are. But what we do honor is our religious friends who have owned that word in their religious world for over 10,000 years and we oppose their being forced, in these modern times, to change the meaning of this word against their will. They have a right to that word. In their scriptures, considered holy by them, our Christian, Muslim, and Jewish friends find their God honoring the covenant between a man and a woman as something special. They, our religious friends, call this marriage. They have been doing so for ten millennia. We respect their convictions and say to those who want them to change: get your own word. "Marriage" belongs to them. It always has, and for as long as they want it to, it will.

"Dad, if two guys can marry each other, does that mean three guys can be married to each other as well? Or how about four?"

"Three, four, ten... it doesn't matter how many guys want to live together. That's up to them. They just can't call it 'marriage.' That word is used to describe something else."

Chapter 25

Pro-Life Guilt

Dumb as a box of rocks...but he was pro-life and wanted my vote.

Conservatives refuse to feel guilty for not voting for a person simply because they share the same view as we do on one important issue. Every election it happens. A number of candidates from both political parties run in primaries and the winners then face off in the general election. Most of the time, the candidates are serious, well-intentioned, and knowledgeable regarding the issues and know what their position is on them. Usually, there is no "perfect" candidate and a choice must be made about who most closely represents our views or positions on a number of issues. And that's where "pro-life guilt" comes into play.

When a person runs for public office and wins, they are given a tremendous responsibility to represent the people of their district in a professional and knowledgeable way. The issues that they need to vote on, once they are in office, should be fundamentally understood by them, prior to entering the race. Of course, very few people fully understand the minor details of every single issue that will come before them, let alone are able to articulate their position on those details. However, they should have some understanding about most issues and they must be able to at least give some indication as to where they stand—except when it comes to the "pro-life" folks.

Here in Michigan, our economy has been racked by the national recession, as well as a precipitous decline in our manufacturing base. The combination of these two events has made the issue of jobs a top priority of our elected leaders in both major parties and these leaders must understand how to create a climate where jobs can grow and flourish. Our state is also home to many great universities and colleges, so our leaders must understand their role in how they should fund, manage, and oversee these institutions. We have a great agriculture sector, science corridor, health care industry and enjoy many natural resources that most states only dream of. Again, how a politician is going to legislate to optimize each of these areas is very important. Unfortunately, every now and then a politician, who is woefully inadequate in terms of understanding even the most rudimentary details of our complicated state, waves the "pro-life" flag and somehow that issue is supposed to make us guilty if we don't cast our vote their way. Conservatives believe that the issue of abortion is very important, but it is not so important that we send unqualified people to represent us in the halls of Congress or the State House.

Let's be clear. Conservatives want it to be illegal for a woman to have the right to terminate her pregnancy prior to bringing the baby to term. We want our politicians to vote that way, and we will take serious note when they don't. But conservatives also understand that the issue of stopping abortion does not rest solely in the hands of legislators and/or the Supreme Court. The only way to stop abortions from occurring is to win over the hearts and minds of those who choose to support this atrocity, either by having abortions or supporting and encouraging those who do. This is why conservatives are a bit sanguine about insisting that every politician we support declares their allegiance to the pro-life cause. If the pro-life candidate is equal to the candidate that supports abortion then it's no contest, we will vote pro-life. If, however they are like the pro-life candidate that I recently met at a Republican gathering who seemed to have the I.Q. of a yellow perch, they will be rejected by the conservatives.

I suppose there are other hot-button issues where both the advocates for and against certain laws somehow think that the entire fate of the country hinges on their one single concern. This is bound to happen when a person has the luxury of ignoring all of the other problems in society and can concentrate solely on the one that is of most concern to them. However, in a large, robust, complicated, and pluralistic society such as the United States, we need smart, articulate, and genuine people elected at every level. If they are pro-life, so much the better; but it's not the controlling factor.

Chapter 26

The Death Penalty

Conservatives believe that the death penalty can be an appropriate sentence and a plausible deterrent for certain crimes.

The debate over the death penalty involves some extraneous circumstances that tend to cloud the real issue. It also contains several irrefutable points that are necessary to acknowledge so there can be an honest assessment. Finally, it's an argument that is more esoteric than practical because both sides know that capital punishment is used so rarely, that the ramifications of winning or losing the debate will have limited effect on society. However, it is an important issue, and one that conservatives believe should be defended where it is used, and advocated for where it isn't.

First let's get the bumper sticker debate off the table right now: "You can't be pro-life and pro-death penalty at the same time." Yes, I'm afraid you can. This argument is usually the first one thrown out by those opposing capital punishment, because if they can get you to contradict yourself, then it's "game over" right away. However, it's entirely possible to be both pro-life and advocate for the use of the death penalty. Here's why. In the case of abortion, there is no due process. If you look at the conservative argument for the rights of the baby, it will always state: without due process. Conservatives oppose the killing of babies, not on the basis of religious beliefs (although they understand this view) nor economic ones (although can you imagine what the positive economic impact would be in the U.S. if all those aborted babies were born?). No, they defend the baby's right to live because babies are not guilty of anything other than being conceived, which in the U.S. is not a crime. This is not true of a convicted murderer. They have gone through due process. They have been accused, tried, and convicted. They are not innocent, they are guilty. Please don't compare these two individuals on the back bumper of your car. It makes you look silly and uninformed.

Second, it has been pointed out to me many times that capital punishment is not a deterrent because the time it takes for someone to go from indictment to the electric chair is years. I've heard it being compared to a seven-year-old child who, if he knew that he wouldn't be punished by his father for something he did in school until after he was out college, wouldn't be deterred in the least. Sadly, this is true—but this is one of those extraneous circumstances that cloud the real issue. (The observation that our legal system is so dysfunctional that it cannot be seen as a deterrent is correct—so let's change the legal system. That's another topic for another day.) Capital punishment may not deter people from contemplating or even committing a crime; but when capital punishment is meted out, it certainly prevents the criminal from committing future crimes.

The third issue is more problematic for the conservative, but it's one that is getting easier to justify by the day. What about wrongful convictions? Can we justify putting one innocent person to death? Shouldn't we suspend the death penalty to protect from this tragedy? No, and no. First, we can never justify putting one innocent person to death. No one is trying to argue that. The person who would be put to death would have been unanimously convicted by a jury, who would have been told prior to the trial that the defendant would be subject to the death penalty if convicted. The level of evidence would be raised to its highest standard (beyond a shadow of a doubt), and the person would have had to exhaust all of their appeals. This is far from some willy-nilly kangaroo court that would convict someone lightly. Suspending the death penalty will not make our court system more or less likely to make a mistake. Better criminal justice investigations and better technology will, and that's where the problem is getting easier every day. In the past, a critic of the death penalty could say that evidence produced through new technologies, such as DNA testing, proves that some innocent people have been put to death—and they may be right. *Now*, however, we *have* DNA testing and other technologies. It is admissible as evidence in a trial, and this is good news because this substantially reduces the possibility of a convicting a person who isn't guilty.

Finally, critics have said that capital punishment is unconstitutional because it causes cruel and unusual punishment, forbidden by the Eighth Amendment. The only problem is, when the Eighth Amendment was drafted, capital punishment was legal and sometimes practiced. If the authors had wished to include it as such, they would have done it then.

Capital punishment is rare today. Many states have outlawed it and others don't have the stomach for it. But as crime gets worse and tragedies such as mass killings become more and more common, someone might want to consider going back to it as a means of making the punishment fit the crime, or trying to deter someone else from committing one in the first place. Conservatives believe that keeping the debate about capital punishment alive and defending it when we can is correct and proper and advances our principles without compromising them.

Chapter 27

Climate Change

Conservatives believe that the climate is changing. They believe it could be man-made, or it could be the natural cycles in nature that have been occurring since time began. It doesn't really matter because we are pragmatists. We deal with the facts as they are and not as we would like them to be. Fact is, the solutions that are being put forth by those who believe they have the answer to this situation are either unilaterally harmful to the United States, or unacceptable to those of us who believe in free markets.

The world has a traffic cop. That cop is the United Nations. Under its authority, there has been a tremendous amount of research done regarding the negative impact of four "greenhouse gases," namely carbon dioxide, methane, nitrous oxide, and sulfur hexafluoride. Once they (the U.N.) believed they had enough evidence that the emission of these gases needed to be curbed (or else the world would heat up and bad things would happen), they called for a meeting. It was held in 2007, in Kyoto Japan, and the agreement reached there is now referred to as the Kyoto Protocol. What the Kyoto Protocol said in general was, "You developed countries are producing most of the greenhouse gases due to your industrialized economies, and we want you to reduce these gases to the levels you had back in 1990. Your poorer cousins haven't had the benefit of industrializing yet, so they don't have to go back to their levels, but they get to emit more than they are now to help them catch up." Huh? This may sound "fair" if you are an undeveloped country, but the United States said "no." The reason that the United States said "no" was that we knew that the economic impact (in terms of lost jobs) that this commitment would have on our economy would be devastating. Second, we knew that because the targets were so unreasonable, other countries that got a big "atta-boy" for signing on would soon be back to the table and wanting to renegotiate. This became a reality when Canada withdrew from the Protocol in 2011. Canada had committed to cutting its greenhouse gas emissions to 6% below 1990 levels by 2012, but in 2009 emissions were 17% higher than in 1990. Environment Minister Peter Kent cited Canada's liability for "enormous financial penalties" under the treaty, unless it withdrew. Russia and Japan have already said that they are not going to take on any new targets either. Conservatives have been pilloried for our lack of support for Kyoto. But in truth, we knew that this would happen and didn't want the United States to be hypocrites by agreeing to do something that we knew we wouldn't be able to do in the first place. In retrospect, this was the best decision.

The second reason that conservatives oppose the Kyoto Protocol is that we believe in market-based solutions. Simply stated, conservatives believe that in the long run, this problem will be solved by a combination of two things—both a product of free markets. First, if the climate is changing as the experts say it is, this will be continually reported in the daily news and, yes, refuted by those who have a legitimate right to do so. This debate will go on for quite some time, and eventually a winner will emerge. Either the experts will win due to their irrefutable evidence, or the critics will be exonerated by the same. But this issue is so huge that it must play out on the global stage and the vast majority of people must be convinced that it is the problem we are being told it is. When this happens, individual attitudes and actions will begin to change. They will make purchases that reflect the need to solve the problem, such as being willing to pay for products that are made in an environmentally sensitive way, or will be more likely to voluntarily reduce or at least control actions that they feel are harmful to the cause. The key here is "voluntarily." People must believe it is in their own long-term interest to do this, and when they do the marketplace will respond by offering products and services that meet their demands. Second, technology is already being focused on improving things that are currently being thought of as environmentally friendly. Better solar panels, electric cars, and wind generators are three examples of products that have undergone tremendous innovation over the past decade. Conservatives applaud these advances, but disagree with the need to subsidize these products with taxpayer monies.

There are those who will argue that this approach takes too much time. They point out that while the debate is going on, the world is warming and really bad things are happening to the environment. This may or may not be true. That is all part of the subject of the debate. If they are right, yes, some damage will be done to the environment that would not have happened if we, as a world population, had acted sooner. But the reality is very few governments are going to unilaterally wind back the clock to 1990, while their people are being thrown out of work. Nor are they going to subsidize the push into "green energy" so fast that they go bankrupt in the process.

The third reason conservatives are sanguine about the solutions being proffered by experts is that this may be a problem where there will be no solution for a very long time. Consider these facts, which appeared in a *New York Times* article dated August

19, 2012 by Elisabeth Rosenthal, regarding air-conditioning and its effect on climate change.

- Fact 1: Nearly all of the world's booming cities are in the tropics and will be home to an estimated one billion new consumers by 2025. As temperatures rise, they— and we—will use more air-conditioning.
- Fact 2: Air-conditioners draw copious amounts of electricity, and deliver a double whammy in terms of climate change, since both the electricity they use and the coolants they contain result in planet-warming emissions.
- Fact 3: Scientific studies increasingly show that health and productivity rise significantly if indoor temperature is cooled in hot weather. So cooling is not just about comfort, it's about productivity and economic vitality as well.

Ms. Rosenthal goes on to state, "*Sum up these facts and it's hard to escape; today's humans probably need air-conditioning if they want to thrive and prosper. Yet if all those new city dwellers use air-conditioning the way Americans do, life could be one stuttering series of massive blackouts, accompanied by disastrous planet-warming emissions. We can't live with air-conditioning, but we can't live without it either.*"

Projections of air-conditioning use are daunting. In 2007, only 11% of households in Brazil and 2% in India had air-conditioning, compared with 87% in the United States, which has a more temperate climate. In this same article Michael Sivak, a research professor in energy at the University of Michigan, states, "There is huge latent demand for electricity. Current energy demand does not yet reflect what will happen when these countries have more money and more people can afford air-conditioning." Professor Sivak has estimated that, based on its climate and the size of the population, the cooling needs of Mumbai alone could be about a quarter of those of the entire United States, which he calls *"one scary statistic."*

Now, would those who chastised the United States for not supporting the Kyoto Protocol suggest that the newcomers to air-conditioning in India and Brazil be denied this convenience? I don't think so. Then what? The "scary statistic" is going to occur, and when it starts to happen, person by person all over the world will understand that they have to take action to avoid a disastrous consequence. One by one we will turn off our air-conditioning units and begin to walk to work and the store, driving less as a result. We will use fewer and fewer products that require greenhouse gases in their production and we will all do this voluntarily. If the problem is man-made, it will slowly be reversed.

Conservatives believe that the climate is changing. We are not ignorant of that fact, but conservatives also believe in the power of people to recognize self-destructive behavior and change their attitudes and habits accordingly, thus solving the problem at hand. This issue is similar to (but of course not exactly like) that of smoking. For years, as a nation, we smoked cigarettes or were tolerant of those who did. Then, as research was done and the harmful effects of smoking were revealed, slowly people started to change their attitudes toward it. Yes, there was a lot of debate on both sides of the issue, but eventually the right side won. Today, society has collectively agreed to change its attitudes and actions in such a way as to reduce this problem to a fraction of what it once was. The same type of process must happen with the issue of climate change.

The rhetoric on both sides of the issue is heated, but this should be expected as the consequences of getting this wrong in either direction could be severe. In reality, many people are already changing their behaviors with their belief that climate change is man-made, and so the problem is being addressed—although perhaps not as fast as some would like.

Chapter 28

Taxes

Conservatives believe they should pay taxes. That issue has never been in doubt. The problem that conservatives have with taxes is that they believe they are not levied fairly, at times they are too high, and once new ones are enacted as law, they are virtually impossible to rescind. Conservatives also believe that everyone with income should pay at least some level of income taxes, regardless of whether it is only a small amount of the minimum wage. (More on that at the end of this chapter.)

Where to start?

At lunch with a liberal friend of mine, I made a statement. "There are three levels of tax rates available to the politicians, and you and I completely agree on the ramifications of two of the three." Now this person and I rarely agree on anything and so she looked a bit unconvinced. I went on, "What would be the ramifications, in terms of revenue collection, if the income tax rate was zero?" "There would be no revenue collected," she said. "Correct," I agreed. "Now, what if the rate was 100%?" "Same result," she replied. "Correct again," I said. "So you see, we both agree that if the rate was zero or one hundred, the result would be the same—no revenue collected." "Yes, I agree," she quipped. "Welcome to the Laffer Curve," I said, and begin to draw an elliptical arch on the paper covering the table.

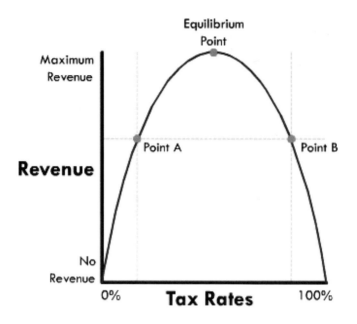

If the tax rate is zero, then no revenue is collected. If the tax rate is 100, then the result is the same. However, starting at zero if the rate goes to 1%, a little bit of tax is collected. At 2% that number goes up again. I won't point out every rate available to the politicians (3, 4, 5, 6, etc.), but at some point the curve starts to go from vertical to horizontal, and if the rate keeps going up, the amount of tax collected starts to go down. This is not an argument over "fat cats" versus the middle class. This is a fact that applies equally to everyone. As your tax rate increases, your desire to earn will go down until at some point it gets high enough that you just quit.

So, what is the appropriate rate? A direct answer would only be an opinion since finding this rate in an economy as diverse and dynamic as that in the United States is impossible. However, my opinion is that once the amount of money the government takes away from you approaches 33%, your appetite to work hard and take risks starts to wane. When that happens the amount of money you send them starts to go down and liberals do what they always do—suggest that the tax rates be raised.

Conservatives believe that there is a direct correlation between the tax rate and the revenue that is raised and that the line is not linear but parabolic, such as is depicted in the exhibit.

Conservatives also believe that everyone, regardless of income, should be required to pay some level of income tax. Allowing a person to work without paying any income tax whatsoever plants the seeds of an entitlement mentality. It also serves to disconnect that individual from the reality that it costs society a lot of money for everyone to be here and that even in some small way everyone should be required to pay his or her part. I know they will howl that they simply can't afford it, but asking them to pay just 1% would help them understand that the rest of us are picking up the bill.

Maybe I'll Just Quit

"If rich guys give more of their pay,
The Treasury coffers then will stay
Full of cash that I can spend
On pork programs that never end"

"What they send now is not enough
To fund my plans, it will be rough.
But if they're punished for their greed
I'll spend with even greater speed."

The President had made it clear
My Tax rate would go up this year
But I already paid a lot.
This growing tax bite had to stop.

Disappointed at this news
I thought, *"Where does he get his views?*
He clearly doesn't have a clue.
But liberal leaders rarely do."

"The Rich" was what he labeled me.
At first I thought, *"How could that be?*
I'm just an ordinary Joe.
He acts like I have lots of dough."

I recognized right then and there
His use of dirty class warfare.
The *"Haves"* his teleprompters say,
"Are greedy, guilty, and must pay."

"And for their crime of thrift and sweat,
The 'Haves' must give the government
A larger portion of their gains,"
To fund his growing gravy train.

It's then a thought popped in my head.
"What if I quit my job instead?
I have a little set aside.
It will be tight, but I'll get by."

"I really do not care to earn
When more and more must be returned.
I think I'll join the other side.
Instead of pulling, I'll just ride!"

When the president was told
That I decided to forego
The need to pay his higher rate
By quitting now, he was irate.

"You tell that man he cannot quit."
He stomped and yelled and pitched a fit.
"I need his money for my plan,
To help the government expand."

"He's very greedy, don't you know
And his decision only shows
He's only thinking of his needs.
I hate to think where this might lead."

It's then he heard that ringing tone
A message on his new smart phone
"URGENT SIR, DO NOT DELAY.
COME TO CONGRESS RIGHT AWAY."

Outside the Congress, crowds appeared.
A tax revolt was in high gear.
The people finally had enough.
They all just quit, it was no bluff.

"Every year we send you cash
And ask you that you make it last.
But every year, you spend it all,
And borrow more, we are appalled."

"Sixteen trillion is the debt.
We don't think you quite get it yet.
'Cause with your budget plans you show
A trillion more each year we'll owe!"

The People said *"Enough's enough.*
We all quit too, this is no bluff.
We want to join the ranks today,
Who ride instead of pull the sleigh."

The bluff was called, the people quit.
And politicians threw a fit.
But that was what it took that day
To change their mind-set and their ways.

The Congress then drew up a plan
To shrink the budget, not expand.
Whole departments were shut down,
And bureaucrats run out of town.

Bloated budgets now in line,
The people's taxes now declined.
And when they did, their HOPE regained.
And that's when things did really CHANGE.

Chapter 29

Tax Havens

The words almost make you shudder. Associated with cloak-and-dagger secrecy, hush money, secret societies, and all-around general suspicion, tax havens have become the target of politicians who feel they are being cheated out of their ability to collect revenue from the profits of people who use them. If someone tries to defend these havens, then they are slandered as being sympathetic to these greedy people and simply not credible.

But conservatives know better. Conservatives believe that as long as a person plays by the rules established by both the U.S. government and the corresponding government providing the "tax haven," then they are perfectly legitimate and allow a person to do with their profits what they wish.

Now, let's look at some facts.

When a person (U.S. citizen or not) makes money in the United States, they are required to pay taxes on that money. When a U.S. citizen makes money in another country, they either have to pay taxes on that money where it was made, or in the United States. What they can't do, under law, is make money in another country, and not pay the appropriate rate in that country, and then not pay any in the U.S. either. Our company has done business in Mexico, Canada, the Bahamas, Argentina, and Jamaica in the past and in every case we either paid the taxes in the local country, or declared the profits here in the U.S. and paid our taxes accordingly. However, what happens when a country does not have any tax on income? Is it legal to send the leftover profit (after paying your taxes) from your business dealings to one of these countries, make money on your investments, and then because that country does not have an income tax, not have to pay taxes on your income? The answer is yes. In fact, this type of tax avoidance is done all the time at the state level here in the United States. Millions of Americans move to states that don't have an income tax for this very purpose. One of the reasons that Florida and Texas have grown like they have over the past several decades is their lack of an income tax. Few people who move to these states for that reason would think of themselves as "tax cheats," but if the definition of making your money in a location that doesn't tax it is applied evenly, then they are in the same boat as the "fat cats" who use tax havens.

Conservatives believe that once you have made your money and paid taxes on those earnings, you should be free to invest them wherever you wish. Being made out to look like some kind of shady character or likened to a social pariah is simply wrong.

Chapter 30

Tax Fairness

Conservatives believe that everybody should be treated "fair." But that's no big surprise; everybody wants to be treated "fair." The desire to not be taken advantage of isn't merely the domain of the poor or disadvantaged; it's felt just as strongly by folks in every spectrum of our society. And contrary to popular belief, 99% of the time everyone is pretty much treated the same. Or, in the words of conservatives, "fair."

Consider the following:

- The tax rate on cigarettes is the same for poor and rich people, and no one argues that it's unfair.
- The tax rate on gasoline is the same for poor and rich people, and no one argues that it's unfair.
- The property tax rate is the same for poor and rich people, and no one argues that it's unfair.
- The sales tax rate is the same for poor and rich people, and no one argues that it's unfair.
- The toll roads charge the same for poor and rich.
- The fee to enter a national park is the same for poor and rich.
- The fee to cross the Mackinac Bridge (here in Michigan) is the same for poor and rich.
- The fee to visit the local zoo is the same for poor and rich.
- The surcharge on hotels and rental cars for targeted city expenditures is the same for poor and rich.

- Speeding tickets are the same for the poor as they are for the rich.
- Tours of the Washington Monument are the same for the poor and the rich.

From essentials such as food, shelter, and clothing, to luxuries such as theater tickets and sporting events, the poor people in this country are treated the same as rich people. No one asks you how much you make before you buy a hamburger at McDonalds. It's not $1.00 if you're poor and $2.00 if you're rich. Everybody is treated the same—fair.

Except for how we are treated when it comes to income taxes. Washington, in its infinite wisdom, has decided that it is "fair" if half the people in the United States don't pay any income taxes, some pay at a 15% rate, some at 25%, and the rest at 34%.

Conservatives believe that this is blatantly unfair for two very important reasons. First, it could be argued, that the poor already get more in benefits from the government than the rich do. Food stamps, Medicaid, low interest college loans or grants, free access to healthcare, and dozens of programs that are targeted to help low-income families are only available to them, and no one is complaining about this. Conservatives, not all rich by a long shot, understand the need for some level of help to folks who are down-and-out and we believe it's wise and compassionate to help them to some extent. To call it "fair" to give them these things and deny it to others would not be an accurate statement. It may not be fair, but we agree with it nonetheless.

Second, the fact that 46% of the people in the U.S. don't pay any income taxes at all is simply and blatantly unfair. This chapter is not about what the ultimate solution to this situation is; that will come elsewhere in the book. But conservatives feel that if you live in this country and enjoy all of the benefits such as police and fire protection, free libraries, free roads, and free municipal parks, you ought to pay at least something. How much? Let's start with 1%. Who could argue with 1%? If a person makes the mandated minimum wage this would mean that they would owe about seven cents an hour in federal income taxes. If they work 40 hours per week, this would mean $2.80 would be due to the government. If that's too much, let's make it 0.5% and their obligation would be reduced to less than the cost of a Big Mac. But I hope you caught the intended use of the word...obligation. That's right; this group that now gets a free pass on income taxes would have an obligation to pay something, no matter how small it ends up being. It's not the amount, it's the fact that they should have to do what the rest of us have to do (in the spirit of fairness, of course), and that is to pay income taxes. Conservatives believe that if everybody had to pay at least something, then for the first time we would all have "skin in the game." For the first time, these people who are currently getting a free ride would perhaps feel obligated to participate fully in society. This may start with them voting (studies have shown that income is the biggest determining factor in whether or not a person votes), and continue by them now feeling empowered to complain about poor public service. Quite honestly, we found out as a society a long time ago that if you get something for nothing, you don't appreciate it nor take care of it as much as you would if you had to pay for it yourself. A second advantage to having them pay something is that the government can start incrementally, over the years, raising their rates. This will also give them a sense of what the rest of us have been experiencing since 1986. For those of you who don't follow these things at home, the tax rate for the highest earners in 1986 was 28%. It rose incrementally to 39% but was mercifully lowered to 34%— where it stands as of the writing of this chapter—in 2004 under President George W. Bush.

Fair. That's all conservatives want. That's what we all want. Describing "fair" may be subjective, but some people paying almost 34% of their income in taxes and others paying nothing can't seem fair to anyone.

"Dad, Tommy's dad thinks you are cruel, mean and heartless because you want poor people to pay taxes."

"Sorry son. It just seems fair to me that everyone who enjoys living here should at least have to pay something."

Chapter 31

The Corporate Income Tax

Conservatives believe that the corporate income tax is a bad idea. A really bad idea.

The accumulation of wealth is the goal of every citizen in the world. I don't mean that every person wants to be rich, but every person wants to have enough to live on and not starve to death. After that, most people would like some clothes and maybe a roof over their heads. Subsequently, there are others who would like enough money to have a hobby, or take some time off to travel. Finally, there are those who, once they have enough to do all that, want even more. They want to build successful companies and help others with the money they have earned. But this wealth, whether small or great, is only gained in one way: through commerce. It is the buying and selling of goods and services between two entities, whether they are individuals or corporations, where profit is earned, and wealth is accumulated.

The reason that conservatives believe the corporate income tax is a bad idea is that it unnecessarily slows and restrains the very vehicle used to produce the wealth of the world in the first place. Second, the corporate income tax is a ruse. Corporations are simply associations of individuals who have pooled their resources to own a company. Without these individuals, a company would not exist. This is true from General Electric to Bob's Plumbing and Heating. Neither would exist if it wasn't for the thousands of shareholders in the case of General Electric, or

Bob in the case of his heating company. Third, a corporate income tax is nothing more than an obligation that the company must pay, similar to a utility bill or monthly rent invoice. It is a cost of doing business that, along with all of the other costs, is added to a corporation's expenses and is covered by its revenue. So in essence, the corporation just passes this cost on to its customers, who then pay more for its goods and services. And fourth, corporations are generally non-political. Their purpose is directed toward profits and not toward fostering some favored political position or even national zeal. And it's this last reason that the United States must eliminate the corporate income tax.

The United States is a mature country, so we don't have millions of people who will work for pennies a day, like China or India do. We have comparative advantages in engineering, design, software development, management skills, medicine, and other such industries that require more and more brains and less and less brawn. For the companies in the United States to grow and prosper, they need to continue improving on their current advantages, but also need to look for other areas where they can be more competitive than their counterparts worldwide. Conservatives believe that if the United States government eliminated the corporate income tax, it would unleash a torrent of economic development that would make the first two centuries of growth this country has enjoyed look like child's play. Think for a moment about that fourth reason above: corporations generally favor profits over politics or even national pride. Now consider the ramifications of what would happen if companies around the world were able to operate in the United States, free of income tax. Would the aircraft company considering a new facility in Montreal now favor Wichita? No question about it. How about the car manufacturer that has facilities in Mexico because of the low labor rates? Operating without an income tax would be more advantageous than people who would even work for free. Those jobs would come back to the United States faster than you can sing Dixie.

I can hear the rebuttal now. *"Washington needs the revenue! You must make these corporations pay their fair share."* If that is what you think, then you would be wrong on both counts. First, Washington would still get its revenue. It's just that now it would come from the individuals who have all those new jobs created when the companies from around the world built their new facilities here. Corporations only contribute 9% of the total amount collected by the government in the first place, but it's still a $200 billion per year drag that could instead be going into research and development or new investments that these companies would make. Secondly, they don't need to pay "their fair share" because "they" are "us." We, the private citizens of this country, own these corporations and we know that any money we pay in taxes both lowers our profits and raises our costs. There is an old saying that comes from the comic strip Pogo, where he wisely pointed out in a situation similar to what we are describing here: *"We have met the enemy, and he is us."* Pogo discovered what many conservatives already know—if you tax corporations, you are only hurting yourself.

The corporate tax rate in the United States is the highest in the developed world. To circumvent this situation Congress has devised hundreds of loopholes, gimmicks and subsidies that make up the three-inch thick book known as the U.S. Tax Code. No one pays the real rate, and the truth is it has gotten so complicated that the temptation to "game the system" using a huge contingent of lawyers and accountants is turning into a regular practice. Let's stop the madness. Eliminate the corporate income tax and things will be very simple. The United States will be the undisputed leader in jobs creation, and our corporations will be the envy of the world.

"Dad, why doesn't the government want to eliminate the Corporate Income Tax?"

"Because once a tax is placed on the people by the government it is virtually impossible for the politicians to eliminate it. In fact, I'm not sure it's ever happened."

Chapter 32

The Flat Tax

Conservatives believe that since everyone in this country is able to enjoy its benefits, everyone should pay income taxes. Poor people and rich people should both pay taxes...and everyone should pay at the same rate. That's only fair.

Conservatives also believe the convoluted system we currently have in this country for determining how much a person owes in income taxes is an abomination. Read these quotes, and note the authors.

"The tax code has become near incomprehensible except to specialists."

Daniel Patrick Moynihan, Chairman
Senate Finance Committee

"I would repeal the entire Internal Revenue Code, and start over."

Shirley Peterson, Former Commissioner
Internal Revenue Service

"Tax laws are so complex that mechanical rules have caused some lawyers to lose sight of the fact that their stock-in-trade as lawyers should be sound judgment, not an ability to recall an obscure paragraph and manipulate its language to derive unintended tax benefits."

Margret Milner Richardson, Commissioner
Internal Revenue Service

Let's face it, our method of calculating a person's income tax liability is a mess. Conservatives believe that trying to fix it by nibbling around the edges or with further tinkering will never address the real issue of fundamental reform. And what should that reform look like? A flat tax. Everyone with an income of more than $25,000 in the country should pay 19% of their income above that level to the federal government in the form of income tax. (There is one exception, which I'll introduce later in this chapter.) Several key changes should accompany the implementation of the flat tax:

- No deduction for interest on your mortgage.
- No deduction for property taxes paid on your home.
- No deductions for charitable contributions.
- No deductions for 401(k) contributions
- No deduction for depreciation

... to name but a few.

This idea is not new. It has been discussed and debated for over 30 years. Two professors, Robert E. Hall and Alvin Babushka, from the Hoover Institution at Stanford University, have done extensive research on this topic and have written many articles in respected trade journals promoting it. A simple search on the internet will reveal their work, or you can go specifically to www.hoover.com for additional information.

The underlying fairness of a flat tax is that it also eliminates the hundreds of "freebies" outlined in Chapter 11 (Subsidies), and more thoroughly detailed in the Joint Committee on Taxation Document published by Congress. It is these subsidies and the thousands of pages that make up the U.S. Federal Tax Code describing how they apply, that cause our system to be open to mischief and abuse.

I can hear the screaming now, coming from both the Republicans and Democrats. *"You can't take these subsidies away; people have come to rely on them both individually and in their businesses. If you take them away, their taxes will go up and I will be thrown out of office as a result."* Not true. Yes, individuals and corporations will lose a whole bunch of deductions that they now enjoy, but look at the new tax rate. It's only 19%. In many cases this rate is substantially less than what people are paying now. I think what the politicians really want to say is, *"You can't take these subsidies away. How will I bribe people to vote for me or get 'fat cats' to give me big campaign contributions if I can't give them subsidies?"* Now *that* I understand, but unfortunately I don't have an answer for them.

Once a flat tax is implemented, we then need one more law to protect it from being watered down by future politicians doing exactly what they are doing now—giving subsidies. So, conservatives believe that once the flat tax is the law of the land, the bill making it so must also contain language that no further exemptions, loopholes or subsides are to be given to individuals or corporations, period. Without this underlying commitment we will be right back where we started, which is a complicated tax code and the need for a team of lawyers and accountants just to figure out what we owe.

Now, for the exception. The Hall/Rabushka plan would allow a person (or family of four) whose income is less than $25,000 per year to escape paying income taxes. They do this for admittedly political purposes, since people below that amount can currently take advantage of the Earned Income Tax Credit and escape paying any income taxes at all. Requiring them to begin paying taxes under the flat tax would be politically impossible to get through Congress, so they allow this one exemption.

Conservatives have long understood the difference between our ideals and reality, but in this area, we have to part company with Hall/Rabushka. As stated in Chapter 30, conservatives believe that if you live in this country and enjoy all of the benefits such as police and fire protection, free libraries, free roads, and free municipal parks, you ought to pay at least something. How much? One percent.

Fair. That's all conservatives want. That's what we all want. Implementing a flat tax where everybody pays at the same rate is inherently fair. If you make a lot of money, you pay a lot of taxes, but you pay at the same rate as the person who makes less. And if you are just getting by, you still must pay something.

It's only fair.

Chapter 33

Economic Incentives

Economic incentives for businesses are fancy ways to describe what most of us immediately recognize as bribes. But this would be too kind. At least with a bribe, you generally use your own money to coerce the other party. Instead, economic incentives are used by politicians to bribe companies into doing something using taxpayer's money. The "arms race" between the states to throw millions of dollars of taxpayer money at highly profitable companies to do something that they are already intending to do is simply outrageous. Conservatives believe that the marketplace should determine where a company will expand or build, and these companies should do so based on market economics, business conditions, and demographics and never because they are receiving a bribe.

I'm in the construction business and I build a lot of buildings for companies who receive economic incentive packages from states all across the U.S. I don't fault these companies one bit for taking advantage of what states are willing to provide. As a business, if someone wants to give you free money, then you owe it to your shareholders to take advantage of every legal means of receiving it. However, it's not the companies that conservatives are concerned about. It's the taxpayers. As mentioned in the previous paragraph, companies are going to grow and expand due to their desire to make profits and take advantage of market opportunities. I have participated in many of these discussions and I can tell you, quite frankly, that where a company decides to go can definitely be influenced by an economic incentive package. However, I have never heard an executive say, "The market for our product is terrible, but we are going to build anyway because we just can't turn down the economic incentives being offered." That doesn't happen. Now here's the final straw. The stronger a company is (meaning the less they need the incentive) the more they get.

The argument that states receive a good return on their investment is debatable. The research I have done indicates that there are just as many winners (Mercedes Benz in Alabama) as losers (Solyndra in California). Even if they were all winners, conservatives would not believe that economic incentives are a good proposition. And the reason has nothing to do with return on investment. The reason conservatives are opposed to states offering economic incentive packages to private companies is that this is not their job. A government should provide basic services to its population such as building roads, bridges, schools, fire stations, and sewage treatment plants. They should work hard to keep their costs low so that their overall tax rates are competitive, if not the lowest in their region. They should educate their workforce and support their higher educational institutions. If and when a private corporation wants to expand or build, they will look at these things and determine if this is where they want to risk their capital. Using the taxpayer's money to bribe them is unseemly and unethical.

Now, as in any "arms race," neither side (or in this case all 50 sides) wants to unilaterally disarm. Indiana is not going to decide on its own to refuse to offer bribes if Illinois, Michigan, and Ohio still do. The answer has to come from leadership in Washington. Here is a prime example of how the federal government can immediately have a positive impact in all state capitals alike, without any of them being upset with this federal intrusion. Tomorrow, Washington could say to the states, "Go ahead, give away the farm if you want to, but if you do offer private businesses any economic incentives to locate in your state versus another, we (Washington) will reduce the amount of revenue sharing your state gets by double that amount." Instantly, the bribes would stop, and states would be assured that if they concentrate on what is important for all the citizens, instead of the few in the communities where a firm would have been bribed to go, then the playing field will be level and the sanity of the marketplace will be restored.

Chapter 34

The Emergency Broadcast System

In 1963 (yes, I was around in 1963), life was very different than it is now. The communication systems that we enjoy today would not only be unheard-of, they were barely conceivable. Cell phones clipped to our belts (with cameras on them, no less) would only be fantasy in a comic strip like "Dick Tracy."

It was during this time that the government decided it needed a way for the president to directly address the American people in a quick and efficient way, in case of war, threat of war, or grave national crisis. The method chosen was the Emergency Broadcast System. But like all government programs that had their purpose in the past, they are awfully difficult to kill, even when their usefulness has long passed.

Today, we are all familiar with the test:

"This is a test. For the next sixty seconds, this station will conduct a test of the Emergency Broadcast System. This is only a test." And then we hear the single mid-pitched tone drone on for what seems like way more than one minute. In the end however, we are assured. *"The broadcasters in your area, in voluntary cooperation with the FCC and other federal, state, and local authorities have developed this system to keep you informed in the event of an emergency. If this had been an actual emergency, you would have been instructed to tune to one of the broadcast stations in your area. This is only a test."*

This would have been appropriate and perhaps necessary in 1963.

Today, however, if the president wanted to speak to the nation, all he would have to do is walk into the White House Briefing Room and announce that in ten minutes he was going to address the country regarding some grave national crisis. In under ten minutes, the following television networks would be flashing "News Alert" in red across their screens: NBC, CBS, ABC, CNN, MSNBC, Bloomberg, FOX, FOX News, HLN, and CNBC—and this would just be the beginning. In seconds, the websites for all of these outlets would contain the message as well.

Now, when this happens, millions of people will start to Twitter, Facebook, and e-mail each other (resulting, of course, in millions of re-Tweets and forwarding). In a matter of minutes, the whole country would be alerted to the fact that an announcement was imminent—and not one single dime of taxpayer's money would have been spent.

Conservatives believe that as society changes, so must the government. However, they know that once a government program is in place, it is nigh unto impossible to kill it. For this reason we appear very skeptical of new programs. Yes, they may solve a problem today, but someday when the problem is solved either through technology or attrition, the old program just keeps chugging along—spending taxpayer money, even though its effectiveness is now highly in doubt. The Emergency Broadcast System is a tiny fraction of the federal budget, but it is indicative of the way Washington works. Conservatives oppose the Emergency Broadcast System because we believe that private for-profit companies will fill the need for this service, and there is no reason for the government to continue this program.

Now back to your regular programming.

Chapter 35

National Flood Insurance

John Wayne once said, "Life is hard, but it's a lot harder if you're stupid." I don't know if he was specifically referring to the United States Congressman who started the National Flood Insurance Program or the ones who have continued to authorize and fund its existence, but the accusation probably fits both cases.

If I could reword Mr. Wayne's statement a bit, it would be, "The government can waste money fast, but it can waste it even faster if it's stupid."

I love to write and most of the time, I enjoy explaining the conservative's position on any given subject, but this time I'm going to step aside and just refer to an article that first appeared in *USA Today* on August 8, 2010, authored by Thomas Frank. Here is an excerpt.

> In Wilkinson County, Miss., a home has been flooded 34 times since 1978.
>
> Extraordinary as the damage may be, even more extraordinary is that an insurer has paid claims every time, required no flood proofing, never raised premiums after a claim and vowed to continue insuring the house. Forever.
>
> The home's value is $69,900. Yet the total insurance payments are nearly 10 times that: $663,000.

It's no surprise that the insurer faces huge financial problems.

The insurer? The federal government.

The National Flood Insurance Program is the nation's main flood insurer, created by law in 1968 as private companies stopped covering flood damage. The program insures 5.6 million properties nationwide and aims to be self-sustaining by paying claims from premiums it collects.

Instead, it's running deeply in the red. A major reason, a USA TODAY review finds, is that the program has paid people to rebuild over and over in the nation's worst flood zones, while also discounting insurance rates by up to $1 billion a year for flood-prone properties.

Along with the huge losses from Hurricane Katrina, the generous benefits have forced the program to seek an unprecedented $19 billion taxpayer bailout.

"If this were a private insurer, it would be bankrupt," said Robert Hartwig, President of the Insurance Information Institute, an industry think tank.

A USA TODAY review of FEMA records found that the owners of 19,600 homes and commercial buildings worth $25,000 or more have collected insurance payments that exceed the value of their property. The records exclude property addresses.

In Fairhope, Ala., the owner of a $153,000 house has received $2.3 million in claims. A $116,000 Houston home has received $1.6 million. The payments are for damage to homes and what's inside.

"It's the ultimate statement on the failure of the nation's strategy to deal with flooding and flood risk," said environmentalist David Conrad of the National Wildlife Federation, who has received FEMA's Outstanding Public Service Award for promoting flood safety. "It does seem to fit Albert Einstein's definition of insanity — to somehow expect something different when you do the same thing over and over again."

USA TODAY also found that the owners of 370,000 second homes and rental houses get huge insurance discounts. Wealthy resort areas such as Hilton Head Island, S.C., and Longboat Key, Naples and Sanibel, Fla., have some of the largest numbers of second homes and rentals getting the discounts.

The program's financial problems reflect a broader government reluctance to restrain benefits. FEMA leaders and some lawmakers have tried to end the premium discounts and the multiple insurance payments, "but there's always been a few in Congress that have had enough political muscle to hold that back," former FEMA assistant administrator David Maurstad said.

The inaction has helped worsen the program's finances. Lawmakers would not approve a bailout "until the program was substantively reformed" to strengthen finances, Maurstad said.

That has added costs. The $17 billion the program borrowed from taxpayers for Katrina claims created such large interest payments that another $1.7 billion had to be borrowed to pay routine losses in subsequent years. Interest payments to the Treasury since 2006 have cost $2.4 billion alone. The program has repaid just $600 million in principal.

Conservatives believe that a person should be free to build anywhere on their own private property that they wish to, but are adamantly opposed to the federal government providing private, for-profit insurance companies the ways and means of offering flood insurance to these people, when the insurance companies know that the risk is much higher than the reward. How much higher? At least $19 billion higher. This madness has to stop.

Thomas Edison once quoted... "*...when Government goes into business it can always **shift its losses to the taxpayers**. Government never makes ends meet—and that is the first requisite of business.*" (Emphasis mine.)

Conservatives are pragmatic and understand that this federal subsidy cannot be stopped overnight or else policy holders will have a reasonable right to cry "foul." But the federal government *can* stop issuing new policies, tomorrow.

Chapter 36

Cash for Clunkers

In 2009, Congress and the Administration ignored market forces and attempted a bold experiment. The CARS Program (Car Allowance Rebate System, a.k.a. Cash for Clunkers) was launched in an effort to stimulate a moribund economy by providing a boost to a couple of car companies the government had big equity stakes in, and save the environment at the same time. With these two goals in mind, they concocted a plan to spend almost $3 billion of taxpayer money by giving folks a cash credit to buy a new car. The plan called for giving willing participants a bribe for trading in an older, inefficient vehicle (a clunker) for a new one. They probably thought, "might as well save the environment along with our investment."

Now that the dust has settled and the Government Accountability Office (GAO) has issued its report, some interesting details are starting to emerge. First, the GAO stated, "The Program achieved its broad objectives, but the extent to which it stimulated the economy and reduced fuel consumption is uncertain." What were the broad objectives? According to the GAO, members of Congress and the Administration articulated two broad objectives for the Cash for Clunkers program. First, help stimulate the economy, and second, to put more fuel-efficient vehicles on the road.

The reason the GAO could say that the experiment was successful was that the outcome was never a measurable goal. The GAO's report repeatedly states that the outcome was uncertain due to the inability to estimate the number of vehicle sales attributable to the program; versus the sales that would have occurred in the absence of the program. In other words, "We don't know what the effect was but we declared that it was achieved and went home." Declaring victory and leaving is a tool often used by the government when they have inserted themselves into a situation, found it much messier than they realized, and retreated. But opinions are one thing. Facts are another. And in the case of the Cash for Clunkers program, they were looking for data in all the wrong places.

No one disputes that 677,842 car buyers received cash bribes totaling $2,853,416. And no one disputes that the new cars that were purchased were more fuel-efficient than the ones that were turned in and destroyed. But this is not the whole story of the Cash for Clunkers program.

As usual, the law of unintended consequences went into effect, and the real story was the economic harm that the program has done to the businesses and people who were gainfully employed keeping the "Clunkers" running and on the road every day. The GAO has the luxury of publishing their report and acknowledging that they simply don't know what the total effect of the program was. But I submit they didn't even look in the right places. For example, I have an old car. Not a clunker by any stretch but old enough to require a regular routine of replacing tires, batteries, light bulbs, mufflers, brake drums, hoses, oil, shocks, struts, and windshield wipers. No, it's not a lemon. It's an old car and I like it, so I maintain it. Now think about the employment opportunities that were squashed when almost 700,000 old cars, in worse shape than mine, were removed from service through the bribe known as the CARS credit. Yet when I read the GAO report it doesn't even mention this portion of the program that they had to have known was destroying untold numbers of jobs. Would this number be hard to quantify? Yes. One would have to look at auto parts stores and "mom and pop" garages to adequately assess the damage. That would be a very hard statistic to come up with. Better to just say, "objective achieved," and submit the report.

The GAO concludes their report saying, "According to federal government evaluations the Cash for Clunkers Program created or retained somewhere between 40,000 to 120,000 jobs." Nowhere in the report, however, have they attempted to determine how many jobs were lost due to the replacement of these older vehicles with new ones that didn't need servicing.

Congress and the Administration are falling all over themselves to try to stimulate the economy and hoping to "create" jobs. However, we had these jobs; and they would still be here today if these geniuses hadn't spent almost $3 billion destroying them.

Many in Washington continue to view the marketplace with skepticism and distrust. They feel that they must "do something" even if they don't know what the ultimate outcome of their actions will be. In the end, the truth is that they often do more harm than good. But more often, rather than learn from their mistakes, they make some vague proclamation about "achieving broad objectives" and go on to the next debacle.

Chapter 37

Social Security

Conservatives believe that a "deal is a deal," especially if their partner in the deal is an entity as large and wealthy as the U.S. government. So when it comes to Social Security, conservatives believe that the promises made to past generations should be honored and paid in full.

Conservatives also believe that promised benefits to be paid in the future will result in one partner (the U.S. government) being unable to pay because it will be broke.

First some background. Believing that people could not be trusted to prepare for their own retirement, save for unforeseen circumstances, or plan ahead using private insurance, President Franklin D. Roosevelt created and implemented what today is known as Social Security.

A better title would have been Monumental Debacle, but that probably wouldn't have passed the political correctness test of the day.

Social Security started in 1935 as part of the New Deal. During that time the United States was in the midst of the Great Depression and I have no doubt that President Roosevelt did what he thought was right by trying to help unemployed or poor people get through incredibly difficult times. However, what he should have done was implement a temporary, short-term program that would have provided the needed help, and then been dissolved. Unfortunately, that's not what happened.

Instead, 75 years later, this program now threatens to cause a financial disaster of, you might say, monumental proportions.

Conservatives do not criticize the millions of people who have paid into the Monumental Debacle, nor those who have received benefits from it over the years. Quite frankly, they had no choice. Except for a few groups, such as the Amish people, everyone was forced to contribute. The problem, as stated earlier, is that the federal government has made so many promises to so many people regarding the benefits that they are entitled to, and the costs of those benefits are going up faster than the taxes being collected to pay for them.

Here's the big picture. The cost of the benefits that the government has promised its citizens under Social Security are going to rise faster and faster due to the large number of "baby boomers" retiring over the next decade. Consider the following:

- The ratio of workers to retirees is changing in favor of the retirees, causing the program to run a deficit.
- In 2009 the program was already in the red, despite expert predictions that this would not happen until 2017.
- Social Security is very sensitive to inflation because guaranteed cost of living allowances are tied to the Consumer Price Index. We are now in a period of low inflation. Higher inflation, that many economic experts are predicting, is lying ahead and will have a very detrimental impact on the deficit that this program will cause.
- The people retiring in 2012 are part of the first generation of workers who will have paid more in Social

Security taxes during their careers than they will receive in benefits during their retirement.

But here's the really bad news. Over the past 75 years, when the Monumental Debacle (sorry about that...Social Security) ran a surplus, where do you suppose the money went? It was used to buy U.S. Government Bonds. That's right. The cash went to Washington where they spent it all, plus $16 trillion more. They (the government) gave us, in the form of the Social Security Trust Fund, IOUs in return.

Now think about that for a second. If the federal government is $16 trillion in debt now, how in the world will it pay back the IOUs that fund the benefits promised to the people? Oh, let me guess—they'll borrow it!

Conservatives believe that a deal is a deal and we can't go back on the promises made to participants in the program in the past. But conservatives strongly believe that the system should be severely curtailed, or perhaps wound down over time. People should be allowed to keep the money that would have been sent into the program and do the responsible thing and prepare for their own retirement using private insurance or savings.

Chapter 38

Universal Healthcare

In the summer of 2012, the United States Supreme Court ruled that the Affordable Healthcare Act of 2010 was constitutional, and this is now the law of the land. Conservatives understand that this act is not the same as universal healthcare, since it leaves some 30 million Americans without healthcare insurance, either public or private. But conservatives also believe that this Act is just the beginning of a transformation, and as it becomes harder and harder for private insurance companies to compete against the government system, eventually we will have to adopt universal healthcare in this country.

So why are conservatives so opposed to universal healthcare? It can't be that we want sick people to die, because we don't. It can't be that we don't want poor people to have medical treatment; because we do. It can't be that we don't like democrats, liberals, or other bleeding hearts, because we do. We have lots of friends who lean left that are good, decent, honest, hard-working folks who think they are right in supporting universal healthcare.

So what is it? Why are we so opposed to this thing?

It's a matter of rights and responsibilities.

Right now, everyone in this country has a right to access our healthcare system, but no one has the responsibility to take care of his or her own health. All upside, baby, and little downside when it comes to paying for it.

For example:

- If I so choose, I can eat five Big Macs per day until my arteries are so clogged with fat that I need bypass surgery to save my life. And you, Mr./Mrs. Taxpayer, must pay for my operation. And when I'm better I can do it all over again, and you will have to pay again.

- If I so choose, I can smoke five packs of cigarettes a day until I get cancer and need treatment to save my life. And you, Mr./Mrs. Taxpayer, must pay for my treatment. And when I'm better I can do it all over again, and you will have to pay again.

- If I so choose, I can drink five pints of Scotch per day until my liver is shot and I need a new one to save my life. And you, Mr./Mrs. Taxpayer, have to pay for it. And when I'm better I can do it all over again, and you will have to pay again.

- If I so choose, I can have indiscriminate sex with multiple partners until I contract HIV, syphilis, or some other venereal disease and need treatment to save my life. And when I'm treated and back on my feet—after Mr./Mrs. Taxpayer have paid the bill—I can do it all over again, and they will have to pay again.

- If I so choose, I can use cocaine, heroin, and crack until I'm worthless to society and need treatment to save my life. And when I'm better I can do it all over again, and you will have to pay again.

- If I so choose, I can drive my car 130 miles per hour (now, *that* I have done) and smash it to bits and while doing so nearly kill myself, needing surgery in order to save my life. And when I'm better, I can do it all over again, and you will have to pay again.

- If I so choose, I can sit on the couch all day, watch TV non-stop, and never exercise a day in my life resulting in an obese body that needs treatment to save my life. And when I'm better, I can do it all over again, and you will have to pay again.

The Declaration of Independence clearly outlines three unalienable rights that we have as citizens. These include life, liberty, and the pursuit of happiness. Does this mean that I can rob a bank and tell the district attorney that he can't throw me in jail because he would be violating my right to liberty? No, he would simply say that my right comes with a responsibility not to break the law. The same thing goes for life and the pursuit of happiness. Just because I have these rights does not mean I don't have the responsibility to follow the law, or these rights will be taken away.

Conservatives believe that the right to healthcare comes with responsibilities. For instance, if a person smokes and is treated for lung cancer, they have the responsibility to quit smoking. If they don't, they lose the right to government-sponsored healthcare. Same goes for drug addiction, morbid obesity, alcohol-related illnesses, and sexually-transmitted diseases. Conservatives are willing to lend a helping hand when someone is down and out. But they are unwilling to continue to pay for self-destructive behavior on the part of those citizens who just want the right, but not the responsibility.

I can hear the howls now. *"This is America, and if I choose to drink, smoke, and have multiple sex partners, that's my business and no puritanical conservative is going to tell me I can't."* That's right, you can choose any lifestyle you wish, but if you do, I am going to choose not to help you.

"Hey, where are we going to come up with this money to pay our doctor's bill?"

"That's not my problem. You should have thought about that before you ruined your health."

Chapter 39

Healthcare Entitlements

Mr. Smith is 97 years old. He's lived a good life, and now his tired old body has reached its end. Surrounded by friends and family, he is asked if he has any last requests. He says "Yes"...

"I would like two new hip replacements, a new left knee, and while you're at it, please look into a heart transplant."

When the family is informed that Medicare will not cover these costs for a man of his age, they are shocked and incredulous.

152

The family meets in private with the Hospital Administrator and a Medicare representative, out of earshot from old Mr. Smith.

"We understand your anger, but we just don't have the money anymore to pay for every procedure that anyone would wish to have. However, since your family is so upset, we would like to propose that if you choose to pay for these procedures out of your pocket, the Hospital will schedule the work for tomorrow."

This little chat changed everything. Yes, they loved their father, but if someone else wasn't going to pay for his healthcare, neither were they. Their shock and anger quickly disappeared, and old Mr. Smith was given the news.

The cartoon is not funny. It wasn't supposed to be. It reveals a deep secret that we all share and none of us are proud of. If someone we love needs healthcare, especially if they are old, we are more than willing to give it to them—as long as someone else has to pay for it. Second, the cartoon also shows how a person who is very old can insist on (and receive) any number of treatments simply because he or she wants them. After all, healthcare is now a right.

Conservatives do not believe that access to healthcare should be a right. We believe it is a privilege, and one that comes with certain responsibilities. But first, one giant clarification: if someone chooses to pay for healthcare using their own funds, then conservatives believe that they have the right to any and all procedures that they request, if they are able to find a doctor to perform the work.

The right to healthcare is very emotional and has turned us into a nation of hypocrites. Who of us are willing to tell a friend or family member they can't have a procedure that may prolong their life or at least make them more comfortable? Not me. I have many friends who have practiced self-destructive behavior for years and every time this abuse results in them needing medical attention I want to scream, "No way!" But since I'm not directly paying for their care, I keep my mouth shut, giving tacit approval.

But by treating healthcare as a right, without the corresponding responsibility to go along with it, the United States has an economic catastrophe in the making. I won't go into the numbers in this book. You have to be living under a rock not to know that our current level of benefits granted through Medicaid and Medicare are going to bankrupt this country in about 30 years. On its current trajectory it will require every dollar of government revenue by the middle of this century. This will leave us with zero funds for anything other than healthcare. Obviously this is not going to happen. So what's the solution? Conservatives believe that if you want the government to fund your health care, in lieu of doing it yourself with your own dollars, then it is not unreasonable for them to establish a few rules and limitations. If you break the rules, you lose the right. If you are outside of the limitations, you lose the right as well. Remember, you are always free to use your own funds to pay for whatever procedure you wish, but if you are using taxpayer funds, then you don't get to call all the shots. So, what should the rules and limitations be?

First, the rules.

- You can't smoke. If you do smoke, you can't have any procedure done that would be associated with the dangers of smoking. You could have hip surgery or bunions removed, but if you have lung cancer, get your checkbook out.
- You can't be morbidly obese. If you are then you can't have any procedure caused by your weight other than bariatric surgery. If you want this procedure, you must show proof that for at least one year your diet was good, and you exercised every day for at least 30 minutes. Diet and exercise would have to be independently confirmed by a third party, so get ready for some observation of your lifestyle. If you don't want this intrusion into your life, get your checkbook out.
- You can't drink excessive amounts of alcohol. If you do, you can't have any procedure done that would be associated with this type of activity. You could get some

skin cancer removed from your arm, but that liver transplant would be out of the question. If you really wanted that liver transplant, get your checkbook out.

- You can't be convicted of a felony in the preceding 36 months relating to violence and have gunshot wounds or knife wounds treated and paid for by the government. Oh, we'll treat you alright, but you will get an invoice, and we will change the law so that you can't bankrupt your way out of these obligations.
- If you have been convicted of using or dealing in illegal drugs in the preceding 36 months, you will not be treated for free for any overdose or treatment relating to drug abuse and have it paid for by the government. Again, you will be treated; it's just that you will also be billed.
- If you have been convicted of driving under the influence in the preceding 36 months, you will not be treated for free for any accident related to drunk driving and have it paid for by the government. Yup, we'll sew you back together again, but you are going to have to pay us to do so.
- If you have been convicted of an assault in the preceding 36 months you will not be treated for any broken bones, bruises, bloody noses, or split skulls and have it paid for by the government. When you leave the emergency room you will have a cast and an invoice.

In all of the cases above, any medication related to your healthcare will have to be paid for by you for the first 12 months of recovery. So, if you want the government to pay for your pain medication, you'd better be responsible for how you live your life.

Now to the limitations.

- Starting in 2013 no one over the age of 110 is eligible for any Medicaid or Medicare assistance. Period. Why 110? Because no one in the United States is 110. If you are 109, then you and your family have a year to save for any procedure you may want to purchase with your own funds.
- Starting in 2014 the cut-off age for receiving assistance will be lowered to 109, and subsequently lowered one year every other year for the next 50 years until in 2062 the cut-off age for Medicare and Medicaid will be 85 years old. Up until 85, a person will be covered. Over 85 you will have to use either private insurance or your own funds.

Sounds cruel doesn't it? But it is actually very fair, because it is not subjective, but objective. It deals with everyone on the same basis and that is their age, not their race, sex, prior conditions, or political persuasion. So, if you are 30 years old in 2013, you have 55 years to save your money. If you are 40, then you have 47 years to do so. Why does the government have to do this? Because on our own, no one will deny any type of coverage to anyone they know, regardless of the circumstances. So, they are left with no choice. If you want the government to take care of you, you have to follow their rules. If you don't follow the rules, get your checkbook out.

Chapter 40

Personal Responsibility

Conservatism has many foundational principles, but in the mix, personal responsibility ranks near the top. Taking personal responsibility for the ramifications of your decisions—rather than blaming society, parents, lack of money, capitalism, or bad habits—is absolutely fundamental to the conservative belief system.

If personal responsibility was taken seriously by all citizens, then the problems in this country would shrink on a scale that would stagger the imagination.

Conservatives believe that it is wrong to force others to pay for the decision of some to not take their responsibilities seriously. By this I mean, take them seriously enough to change self-destructive behavior, and stop expecting society to continue to fund their reckless behavior.

Unfortunately, over the years and little by little, millions of Americans have become accustomed to having someone else "bail them out" of their lack of personal responsibility. At first, we were told that some people had bad upbringings so we shouldn't blame them for their problems. Others had poor self-esteem, and we needed to give them extra consideration; some had attention deficit disorders; others, poor schools; more still had never been "given the opportunity" that we had, whatever that means. Eventually, we wound up where anyone with any excuse is expected to be able to claim that they are powerless to take personal responsibility for their actions.

Conservatives believe that everyone is responsible for their own actions regardless of their circumstances or lot in life. To allow someone to say, *"I just can't be responsible for myself"* would deny the fact that life has dealt millions of people a bad hand and millions have responded by taking seriously their responsibility to act properly and correctly in society.

Today, there are thousands of men in jails, paid for by you and me, because their fathers did not fulfill their responsibility to raise them into proper adults. There are millions of mothers who are struggling to make ends meet because some dad decided to "move on." The aid these women receive comes from you and me, not the deadbeat dad. There are millions of people who will be scarred forever due to someone drinking and driving. There are 100 million Americans who have to pay more taxes this year because of those who cheat on their taxes. That's right; you pay when someone else cheats. There are subcultures in our communities that glorify violence, crime, rebellion and disrespect for authority. This has resulted in untold billions of dollars spent by you and me fighting crime, drug trafficking and gang behavior. For the conservative, it is very difficult to listen to all of the excuses given for these problems.

We know that if people took their responsibilities seriously, these problems would be virtually eliminated. Think about that. Eliminated. Those are the facts. In the meantime, however, we will continue to pay again and again and again, while the excuses are repeated again and again and again.

Chapter 41

The Designated Hitter Rule

How in the world could there be a conservative position on the designated hitter rule?

Well, there is.

I love baseball. You don't have to love baseball to be a conservative. But if you are a conservative, you believe that the designated hitter rule is a bad rule.

First some observations about the game itself. Baseball is different than other sports. It seems either people love the game, or don't care for it at all. For those of us who love it, it is the most graceful, fluid, artistic, and intellectual of all the major sports. Baseball is different for many reasons, but a few of them are obvious. It doesn't have a clock. The leader of the team is called the manager, when all the other sports call their leaders "coach." The manager wears a uniform, just like the players. Every single outfield is different in every stadium. And finally, there's the history, and oh! what a history it is.

Baseball has been called a "game of inches." And that's true. The result of a game can turn on one pitch thrown just one inch low. It's been called a "thinking man's game," and that's true as well. The strategy that goes into every single pitch is maddeningly complex. For instance, with a runner on first, and the risk of a steal imminent, should the pitcher risk throwing a changeup pitch to a batter (with advance knowledge that the batter has trouble hitting a changeup), understanding that the slow ball speed will raise the likelihood of a successful steal? This is one simple example of one small bit of strategy that each of the nine players has to contend with on every play. Baseball has been called "the national pastime," and arguably it is, with over 60 million people attending games every year.

But it is the mystery of baseball that so intrigues me, and it's why conservatives feel that if you mess with this game too much, it might destroy something that is very delicate and in perfect balance. "Where's the mystery?" you ask. Consider this: when you watch an old film clip of a baseball game from, say, the 1920s, you will see men who look much different than today's athletes playing the game. Babe Ruth comes to mind. He is big, slow, and would never make the roster today in that condition. And when Ruth hit a ball to the third baseman, he was thrown out at first base by a half step. Fast-forward ninety years to today. The runners look like track stars, able to leave ol' Babe in the dust. But when they hit the ball to the third baseman, they are thrown out at first by a half of a step. The distance from home plate to first base is magical: 90 feet. If it were a few feet longer, the game would be woefully out of balance in favor of the defense. A few feet shorter, and the offense would dominate. But 90 feet was the perfect distance in 1920, and still is today. The distance from home plate to the pitcher's mound is 60 feet, 6 inches. In this distance a pitcher must fool a batter into swinging and missing, or not swinging and allowing a strike to occur. Doing this involves throwing a variety of pitch types including fast balls, curveballs, sliders, sinkers, changeups, or knuckleballs. The magic of 60'-6" is that this is the distance where the ball moves the most. Any shorter and the ball wouldn't have begun its movement yet and the batter would clobber it out of the park, any further and the movement would have already occurred and the batter would

162

clobber it as well. But 60'-6" brings the advantage back to the center with neither the pitcher nor the batter having the advantage. "Well," you may say, "they just moved the distance in and out until they found the perfect distance and *voila*, no magic there, just trial and error." But you would be wrong. The distance was established in the mid-1800s when pitchers threw much slower, and the balls behaved much differently due to how they were made and condition they were in. (Sometimes one ball was used for a whole game!). But 60'-6" worked in 1850, and one hundred and sixty years later, with pitchers throwing 100-mile-per-hour tailing fastballs and curveballs that seem to fall off an invisible table, it still does... at 60'-6." There is something mysterious about this game, I tell you.

Now to the designated hitter rule. As I said, baseball has a long history, and the game itself is full of mystery. What it doesn't do well is change, and that is the beauty of it. When it is changed, it upsets a balance that has been in place for over 200 years. In 1977, the guardians of this game got antsy. They saw the sexy high scoring action going on in professional football and tried to "jazz things up a bit." They thought they should bring more excitement with more scoring, and so they decided to let the pitchers in the American League sit on the bench when it was their turn to bat, allowing the manager to designate a hitter to take their swings. (Pitchers usually aren't very good hitters.) At first it worked. Scoring in the American League jumped. Year after year, for twenty years, the National League was outscored. But slowly things began to change, and starting in 1978, and every year since, the National League scores surpassed the American League and its big, strong designated hitters. Something mysterious took place in baseball—something no one could explain, but since 1998 the National League has outscored the American League every year. It's as if the game itself has pushed back against this rule and on its own has mysteriously taken its intended purpose away.

Baseball drips with tradition. Inserting the designated hitter rule into the game in only one of the two leagues screws up the statistics of the players (can a pitcher who has to bat and run the bases be compared to one who doesn't?), and doesn't do a thing for attendance as the National League fills its stadiums to a 72% capacity while the American League number is 65%. Conservatives believe that the designated hitter rule was a bad idea in 1977, and still do 35 years later. Only now we have data to prove our point.

"Dad, when I grow up, I want to play shortstop for the Detroit Tigers."

"That sounds great to me son, but if I was you, I'd still study hard and get a college degree. You know, just in case that baseball thing doesn't work out."

Chapter 42

Private Courts versus Public Courts

Conservatives believe in limited government, but we also believe in efficient and responsive government. For this reason, we are constantly asking ourselves important questions regarding the government's role in our lives. For instance, when Apple thinks Samsung has infringed on one or more of its patents, why does the government have to provide a taxpayer-funded venue for them to "duke it out?" In other words, why is the government in the civil court business in the first place?

Whoa...wait a minute. Don't rush to judgment on this. Please hear me out.

The American legal system is divided into two parts: civil and criminal. The criminal court system is where the government prosecutes criminal activity such as robbery, murder, assault, white-collar crime etc. Conservatives believe in limited government, and going after bad guys is one of the things the government is good at and by all means should do. But what about civil cases such as divorces, landlord-tenant matters, probate, name change, child custody, and lawsuits between businesses? All these civil disputes have something in common: public safety is not a concern, and generally the public has no interest in the outcome. So why is the public being asked to pay?

Today our courts are jammed. One of the reasons they are backed up is the fixed amount of infrastructure that is available to adjudicate cases. For instance, how many courthouses does your county have? One, just like mine. Inside this courthouse is a fixed amount of courtrooms (more for large counties, fewer for small ones; but still a fixed amount). How many judges work at this courthouse? Again, more for large counties, and fewer for smaller ones, but in any case it's a fixed amount. How many hours a day are they open for business? More than likely around eight hours. So what happens when, for some reason, the number of civil lawsuits that are filed on any given day are more than the courthouse can handle? Things start to back up. What happens if they back up for a long time? Then someone decides that we need more courtrooms, judges, and all the personnel that go along with them such as clerks, stenographers, and, security guards, etc. Who has to pay for all this? The taxpayers. Why?

Conservatives like to ask the "why" question a lot. Most of the time, there is a reasonable answer because over time society generally does most things right, and even if the answer doesn't suit our liking, at least we understand the logic of the argument; but not in the case of civil courts.

Providing a venue for civil action between two private parties could be a great for-profit business, and one that could be done while not hurting the integrity of the court system in any way. How might this happen?

First of all, judges would not work for the government, but would be employed on an hourly basis by private corporations. These judges would qualify for the position by being elected by the public in the same manner that they are now. However, we would elect a few more than needed, so that when the inevitable rise in cases comes along, they can be handled efficiently and economically. If the judges do a good job we re-elect them, just like we do now; if they don't, we don't. Instead of one courthouse, these businesses could have several smaller ones in rented commercial spaces (where property taxes are paid, unlike the courthouse!) spread around the county. They would be close to where they are needed and the citizenry would not have to travel very far to seek justice. The stenographers, security staff, and receptionists would not be civil servants with government pensions and benefits, but employees of private companies. How would we choose these private companies? Just like it's done in the marketplace, by competitive bid. Companies would be retained to adjudicate these cases and charge a fee to the plaintiffs who bring them. If a company does a poor job, we do what we do in the private economy, we fire them. If they do a good job, we retain them. What about safety, you might ask? Safety in a civil court is not an issue, it's in the criminal courts where people come in wearing jump-suits and handcuffs. What about juries? Fortunately, most civil trials don't use juries. The judges themselves hear the case and decide the outcome. If a jury trial is needed, the company could be deputized to select jurors from the community and the plaintiff or defendant (whoever requests the jury) pays an additional fee for this service.

Now before you think this idea is un-workable, I would suggest a little trip down to Weston, Florida. Incorporated in 1996, Weston sits on 27 square miles in southern Florida, just north of Miami. It has 63,000 residents, and nine employees. How does it do this? By outsourcing almost all of its municipal functions to private, for-profit companies. This includes police, fire, emergency medical, planning, zoning, engineering, public works, parks and recreation, building codes, solid waste disposal, recycling, accounting, and information technology. None of the 400 men and women is a direct Weston employee, except for the nine senior managers that oversee these private enterprises. If you can be rescued from a fire by a private company, you can sure have your divorce done by one as well.

Conservatives believe in limited government. But we are not in favor of simply complaining without providing solutions. Overcrowding of the court system is a problem. Privatizing the civil side, with the appropriate restrictions in place, will save taxpayer dollars and make the entire system more efficient. So the next time Apple sues Samsung, you can say, "Knock yourselves out, boys, it isn't costing me a dime." Unfortunately, right now it is. This case is not hypothetical—it's happening right now in the summer of 2102. Can you imagine that the world's most valuable company is using our tax dollars to sue its competitor? Maybe this isn't such a bad idea, eh?

Chapter 43

"Loser Pays" Tort Reform

Conservatives believe that when a person sues someone, if they lose, they should have to pay the legal costs of the winning side. This is typically called the "loser pays" system and would go a long way toward reducing the total number of lawsuits in the country, as well as limiting the number of frivolous cases.

Here's why. If you are wronged by another party, you have two choices. One, you can accept the fact that you have been wronged and go on with your life; or two, you can initiate a lawsuit. If you chose the first, you will know the total amount of your loss because you will have just experienced it. That's it. You won't lose any more time, energy, or money. You will simply live with the fact that you were wronged and you will go on. However, if you choose the latter and attempt to recoup your losses in court, the outcome will be much more complicated. First, if you win you will recoup your losses, but you will have to pay your attorney fees, which in many cases can add up to an amount close to the total of your award. Second, if you lose, you will not receive any award, but you will still have to pay your attorney. This can be a very expensive proposition. So, what happens in real life? In many cases, neither. Instead of accepting your losses and walking away, you can hire an attorney "on contingency." This means that if you lose, you don't have to pay anything, including his or her attorney fees; but if you win, he or she gets a cut. You don't really have any skin in the game. Because of this, thousands of

169

lawsuits are brought to court every year by lawyers who are trying to profit from someone else's misfortune. Good for them. This is America and under our capitalist system they are free to make money any way they wish (as long as it's not illegal) and conservatives applaud them for doing so.

However, this comes with a huge downside. Because the lawyers do this for a living, and because they are very good at getting juries to see their clients' plights, they bring many lawsuits that are marginal in the hope that "some of them stick." Often the defendant (the person being sued) is a small business and they are now forced to either settle out-of-court for an agreed-upon sum (this is the lawyers' favorite outcome because they still get their cut but don't actually have to spend very much time on the case), or spend large sums of money defending their innocence.

I own a construction company. We had an employee once who was on a roof when a big wind came up. The employee fell over because of the wind, but did not fall off the roof. It was very scary for him but he did not sustain any bodily injury. A couple of weeks later, we received a letter from his attorney stating that the employee was going to sue for mental distress that he suffered and suggested that we settle out-of-court for $35 thousand. When we questioned the attorney as to how he came up with this amount he candidly admitted that our firm will probably have to pay in the neighborhood of $50 thousand dollars to defend ourselves so getting off with just paying $35 thousand now, and cutting our losses, would probably be a pretty good deal for us. I wanted to throw up.

In another case, I received a complaint from a person who happened to live across the street from where we were constructing a new facility. Yes, the weather had been dry but we were regularly using water trucks to dampen the dirt so that the amount of dust in the air was kept to a minimum. One day, I received a note from this person's attorney stating that we were going to be sued for a tidy sum because his client had to clean his house and car multiple times due to the dust that was blowing onto his property. He sent me pictures of the dust on the car and even inside the house. I felt we were probably guilty (he had pictures, right?) and was resigned to pay whatever the costs were until I got a call from my superintendent who worked on the site. He said that he stopped by the job one night and took a video of the person who was planning to sue us; driving a car on our site in big circles very fast so as to stir up as much dust as possible. Given the direction of the wind, the majority of the dust was headed right for his house. When confronted with the facts, the attorney refused to back down. He knew his client was in the wrong, but he also knew it would cost me a bunch of money to defend myself. He suggested that we settle for an amount slightly less than what he thought our attorney fees would be. If I could have reached through the phone, I would have punched him right in the nose.

"Loser pays" reform would put an end to this kind of nonsense. Critics complain that such reform would prevent many people who cannot afford an attorney from bringing legitimate claims to court, but I disagree. If they truly have been harmed, they can still hire an attorney on a contingent basis just as they can now. It will, however, prevent the current abuse of the system as we have it. Also, "loser pays" only involves civil courts. If a person is harmed in a criminal way, then the local district attorney will still be involved at no cost to the alleged victim.

The ultimate winners in "loser pays" reform are the thousands of small business owners who would now be able to concentrate on building their enterprises, hiring workers, and generally improving the life of all Americans. As for the attorneys... well, they always seem to land on their feet.

"Dad, what's the problem with telling lawyer jokes?"

"Well, lawyers don't think they are funny, and no one else thinks they are jokes."

Chapter 44

Head Start

Conservatives are compassionate people. Conservatives believe that if someone is in need, then they should be given a helping hand. With that said, conservatives are not naive. We know that many times people are in need due to their own repetitive, self-destructive behavior and that continuing to help them will only perpetuate the recipient's reliance on the help—and ultimately it may morph into a powerful sense of entitlement.

However, there is one group of needy people who, through no fault of their own, find themselves hungry, alone, rejected, and otherwise hopeless. These are the kids whose parents are not able, for whatever reason (some legit, some not) to care for them as they should. This chapter is not focused on the cause of their need, but rather on a government solution that has gone awry.

Started in 1965, the federal Head Start Program was initially intended to teach low-income children, in a few weeks during their summer vacation, what they needed to know to start kindergarten. Fast forward 47 years and it is now a huge government-run program with an annual budget of $8 billion, helping around one million kids. Recent studies of this program have produced some alarming results. People who are by no means conservative have started to ask some tough questions and the answers are not necessarily flattering to the program. First, the results of a recent study showed that the positive effects of the program were minimal and vanished by the end of the first grade. Second, the graduates performed about the same as students of similar income and social status who were not part of the program.

Something has to change when even people who believe in government-led solutions are beginning to wonder about its effectiveness. So, just like the Army officer in *Casablanca*, the current administration is shocked—just shocked—at the report and promises that the nation's local Head Start programs would be reviewed over the next three years. In other words, study the problem until your critics get tired and move on, and no one will have to change a thing.

I'm not a math expert, but if I divide $8 billion by one million kids, isn't this $8,000 per kid? Our local public school system educates high school students for $7,500 per kid, and they need a huge building with a gymnasium, track field, band room, science lab, library, and even a pool to do so. It would seem to me that educating a four-year-old for the same amount of time should cost a fraction of that. What's the difference between these two delivery methods? One is controlled at the local level and the other from Washington, D.C.

Conservatives believe that disadvantaged kids need a boost. They also believe that there are for-profit organizations that are already in the business of educating kids and they could do a better job at a lower cost. These businesses run charter schools and day care programs all over the country and they should be allowed to bid on the Head Start Programs. If they can produce the service better and cheaper than the federal government, then that is the route we should take.

But first we have to wait for that three-year study to be completed. Oh yeah, good luck with that.

Chapter 45

Public Funding for Art

Imagine, if you will, how repugnant and nauseating it would be if someone made a small statue of your mother, and then took a picture of this figurine submerged in a bottle of urine. The depth of anger that would well up within you would seem to justify almost any retribution on your part, against this so-called artist. Now, for the next blow. Suppose you were forced to pay the artist to do this.

This simple example is not entirely made up. It happened in the late 1980s when an artist named Robert Mapplethorpe produced a piece of art where the visage was Jesus Christ, not your mother. The medium was the same.

Welcome to the world of the public funding for the arts.

Conservatives believe that art plays a very important part in our lives. We believe that in both primary school (elementary levels) and secondary school (high school levels), art classes are important and should be funded along with other traditional subjects, such as math and science. However, once a student has graduated from high school, if they feel that they would like to learn more about art, or even pursue it as a career, then they should be required to pay for this continuing education with their own money, just like they would have to if they were going to further their studies in any other field of endeavor.

Conservatives believe that requiring the government to fund a highly personal and potentially divisive issue such as art is asking for trouble in the first place. Who should decide whom to fund? What is obscene and what is not? What is worthy of the funding and how much should be given? All of these questions raise the bigger question—why fund it at all?

Let's be clear. Artists should be paid. But they should be paid in the same way a plumber is. They should produce a product that the marketplace wants to buy and then sell it to the highest bidder. This bidder may be a private individual who just happens to like a certain artist's style or technique, or a museum that would like to display an artist's work as part of their collection. In either case, private dollars are being used and not public money, eliminating the need to decide what is acceptable in the public's eye or what is too extreme or obscene to be funded by the taxpayer.

Is this a "tempest in a teapot?" Is it really a big deal? Since 1990, the U.S. government, through the National Endowment for the Arts, has given three thousand one hundred forty-five million taxpayer dollars (that's over $3 billion) to artists and art organizations. Conservatives believe that the private marketplace is where art should be funded and not through government coffers.

Chapter 46

Public Financing of Sport Stadiums

We must just look like suckers. How in the world could multi-million dollar monopolies, which pay their employees multi-million dollars salaries, get the local taxpayers to build them a building so they can conduct business?

Oh, I think I know—because they lie. Declaring an existing facility too old or small, or lacking enough luxury boxes or suites to field a competitive team, they start the extortion process. At a party or not-so-private gathering, they let the fact slip that some other town will build them a new stadium if we won't. This little tidbit is usually dropped when a local newspaper reporter is around so that the public is informed of this "other city option" by a reputable source. The newspaper usually has a sports section, and losing the team would really hurt revenue, so with all the sincerity of a con artist, announce that they (the newspaper) are actually in favor of the deal. Close on the heels of this announcement comes the rosy predictions of construction jobs, spin-off developments, and what a great tool for economic development and neighborhood revitalization this will be, all in one. What a deal.

The practice of professional sports profiting at the expense of taxpayers is not new. Before the stadium gambit, there was the tax shelter dodge in which the purchase and reorganization of a team could generate up to five years of losses, which could then be used to offset the new franchise owner's income from other ventures. When that perk was eliminated, franchise owners would hide behind local governmental units who would issue bonds for them to use the proceeds of to build stadiums. These bonds were municipal bonds and so were exempt from federal income tax. When that gig was up, they just replaced it with explicit solicitation and coercion.

In an extensive study chronicled in the *Journal of Policy Analysis and Management* (what, you don't read that every month?), Dennis Coates and Brad Humphreys made a deep dive into the myth of economic growth caused by new stadiums being built in downtown areas. Contrary to the rosy picture that most community leaders paint, regarding jobs and quality of life improving, their study found this not to be true. In addition to this, the "multiplier effect" which says that for every job created there is a multiple of other jobs that spin off or are created due to the earning and spending power of the original job is also refuted.

First, the multiplier effect. It goes something like this. If a person is hired to work at a stadium, he will need to eat somewhere (restaurant workers get jobs), sleep somewhere (apartments get built), and do a bunch of little things like wash his clothes (laundry workers), go to movies (theater workers), and perhaps even need some new appliances (retail workers). So, in the end, the franchise owners can count all of these additional jobs in their pitch for public money as well. Unfortunately, as pointed out in the Coates/Humphrey study, "The methodologies used by impact studies that gauge the multiplying effect are flawed." Here's why. Let's take our stadium worker who now has a job because of the sports team that plays in the city. Yes, people who want to see a game have to buy tickets (which can cost a small fortune) to the game, and a portion of the ticket prices pass through to our stadium worker, and then all of the multiplying I described above takes place. But aren't we forgetting something here? The person who bought the ticket doesn't have their money any more. And because of this, they can't buy something else. And whatever that "something else" would have been (had they not bought the ticket) would have resulted in additional jobs as well, just like our stadium worker. And yes; those jobs would have multiplying effects as well.

This same argument holds when the public is asked to finance the construction of the stadium itself. When hundreds of millions of dollars are taken out of the paychecks of local taxpayers to pay for the construction of a stadium, those dollars cannot be used elsewhere. If the money is borrowed, through the issuance of public bonds, then the cash doesn't immediately come out of their paychecks, but the taxpayers are on the hook for the loan. This will lower the municipality's ability to borrow for other legitimate functions such as roads, bridges, and infrastructure. What an incredible irony, that the stadium gleams in the sun while the roads, subways, and bridges leading to it crumble.

The Coates/Humphries study concludes with the following outcomes:

- Professional sports stadiums in 37 metropolitan areas that they studied *had no measurable impact on the growth rate of real per capita income.*
- The professional sports stadiums had a statistically significant impact on the level of real per capita income in the same 37 areas, and the *overall* impact was negative.

Conservatives believe that if franchise owners think owning a stadium is such a great deal, then they should risk their own money and build them. If they do, we as the public, will be more than glad to finance roads, subways, bridges and other infrastructure that will not only support their new playground, but all of the other buildings in the city as well.

So, in the end, franchise owners shouldn't lie to us. They should simply state the truth. *"I want people to spend their money on my team, rather than spending it somewhere else. I win, and someone else loses."*

That is the truth.

"Don't worry, after it's built, the whole city will be better off...or at least I will."

"Hey, why should I have to pay for your stadium?

Chapter 47

Eminent Domain

Conservatives believe, and the Constitution affirms, the right of federal, state, and local governments to take a person's private property, compensating him or her fairly, to be used for public use. Ahhh... but what is the meaning of the words, "public use?" Here is where things get a bit dicey; the ramification of the answer has profound consequences.

In the early days of our country, land was abundant. When the government needed some land to build a road, bridge, or canal, there were plenty of places to do so, and it was easy for the people who owned the land on which these things were built to simply relocate nearby, and no one was hurt by this action. However, as the country developed, and space to build infrastructure became more and more limited, the government started to run into some trouble. It was with this in mind that the framers of the Constitution, as well as the drafters of subsequent Amendments, gave the Government the right of "eminent domain," which is basically the unilateral (one sided) right to buy any piece of property (compensating the land owner fairly, of course) for the purpose of public use. From the mid-1700s until the late 1800s, "public use" was pretty much understood to be government-built infrastructure such as the aforementioned roads, bridges, and canals, but soon it started to include things such as utilities (i.e., water, sewer, gas, electric). In 1832 the Supreme Court ruled that eminent domain could also be used to allow a private business, in this case a mill owner, to expand his dam and operations by flooding an upstream neighbor. The court opinion stated that public use does not have to mean public occupation of the land; it can mean a public benefit as well.

So "public use" has now been expanded to "public benefit." "No big deal," you say. Probably not for most of the public, but for the upstream neighbor, I think the expansion of the right of eminent domain had quite an impact, as he now had a lake where he wanted a pasture.

In 1905 the Supreme Court ruled a farmer could expand his irrigation ditch across another farmer's land because that farmer was entitled to "the flow of the waters of the said Fort Canyon Creek ... and the uses of the said waters ... for a public use." Here the Court indicated that the farmer *not* adjacent to the river had as much right as the farmer who *was* to access the waters. I think you can see where this is going. The government is now sticking its nose into private property rights decisions, repeatedly using the excuse "public benefit or public good" to justify it.

Fast forward to 1954. After years of urban development, parts of Washington D.C. were getting pretty ugly. These "slums" held blighted structures, poor people, and high crime. They were also full of private properties. In spite of this fact, the government decided, and the Supreme Court concurred, to take the properties through eminent domain and after taking them and knocking the buildings down, sold the parcels to private redevelopers who would construct condominiums, private office buildings and a shopping center. To be blunt, the government forced private property owners to sell their land to them (the government, using taxpayer money) so that they (the government, using taxpayer money) could knock the buildings down and resell the property to a different set of private property owners. All this was done under the guise of "public use" or "public benefit."

Now we come to the twenty-first century, and the public is starting to reach a tipping point in the government assault on private property rights that conservatives reached 120 years ago. This happened when the Supreme Court affirmed the authority of New London, Connecticut, to take non-blighted private property by eminent domain, and then transfer it for one dollar a year to a private developer solely for the purpose of increasing municipal revenues. Yep, that's right, poorly developed property doesn't bring in as much tax revenue as the nice stuff, so the city of New London decided to fix this problem. This 5-4 Supreme Court decision received a lot of press and for the first time, the average Joe started to ask some critical questions regarding the proper role of government in this type of situation.

Conservatives are often portrayed as grumpy naysayers who always seem to be against progressive government initiatives. This is simply not true. We aren't grumpy. We do, however, understand that there are certain things that government should do, and other things that it should not. Building roads, bridges, and infrastructure is something that they are good at and something they should do (using the power of eminent domain). Circumventing the marketplace and developing real estate with taxpayer money is something they should not.

By the way, do you know how that New London, Connecticut deal turned out? Not so well. After spending $80 million of the taxpayer's money, the property still sits empty, although it has sold to a private concern for $55 million. So much for bringing in higher tax revenue, huh?

Chapter 48

Environmental Protection

The topic of protecting our environment is large and complex and controversial, to say the least. It is on the same level as the economic and social issues about which conservatives have strong convictions. In the debate regarding the proper use of our environment, many times conservatives are labeled as "anti-environment, careless polluters, and wanton destroyers of the planet." In fact, conservatives have a very high regard for the environment and understand that strong measures must be taken for its protection.

However, there is one fundamental difference that exists between liberals and conservatives on the subject of the environment. Liberals generally believe that the environment should be protected from the influence of humans, believing that the preservation will provide more advantages to current and future generations. Conservatives believe that the environment is here for a purpose; to be used in a prudent way now to advance our quality of life. This is a very important difference: preserved versus used.

First, conservatives are pragmatists. We understand that most decisions in life come with a cost. The reality of this was evident here in Michigan recently where our governor held a high-profile press conference, touting the construction of a new factory in a Detroit suburb that was going to make advanced batteries for the auto industry. Hundreds of politicians and local leaders showed up as the governor boasted of how much the

State of Michigan was going to subsidize this private company through bribes—excuse me, economic incentives—paid for by the taxpayers. The batteries were high-tech alright. But the metal needed to make them was fairly mundane. It needed to be mined from the ground, and that was a problem for our governor. Because you see, the northern part of our state, referred to as the Upper Peninsula (or U.P., as we like to call it) contains precisely this material. And, responding to this opportunity to make money, a mining company applied for a permit to dig it up, and send it to Detroit where they would turn it into the aforementioned batteries. Unfortunately, the Governor didn't like that part of the deal. She wanted the "high-tech" part. She loved the scientists, engineers, and white collar workers that would get jobs. She loved the "clean rooms" where the batteries would be made. But in order to have these jobs, someone would have to clear some trees and dig up the ground. The result? The governor delayed the permit for months, only agreeing to it when the irony of the situation was just too much to overlook anymore. This happens all the time.

Second, conservatives don't believe in the theory of "out of sight, out of mind" when it comes to regulating the use of the environment. This hypocritical position happens when a person enjoys the benefit of using a product but would never support environmental destruction necessary to make that product in their own home town. If it's made where they can't see it (preferably in a poor, third-world country) and they never have to approve of the destruction of the environment, then they are just fine. This would be the case if the aforementioned mine was not in Michigan. If it was in India, then the governor would never have been troubled. Many industries are gone, and thousands of jobs have been lost because U.S. manufacturers have simply moved to other countries to make the same goods they were making here, and then shipping them back for us to buy. It doesn't take a genius to figure out that when this happens, the overall global environment doesn't improve, and eventually our trade balance with those countries will become completely out of whack. (Think China.)

Third, conservatives don't hate the Environmental Protection Administration (EPA). In fact, the opposite is true. Our water and air is cleaner today than it has been in decades due to the rules and regulations put in place by Congress and enforced by the EPA. But what we do object to is when the EPA advocates for a position on a given environmental situation, and, knowing that they would never be able to get Congress to pass a law favoring their view, sets up "guidelines" that companies must follow without ever needing the legislature's vote. This type of "mandating without legislating" was recently struck down in West Virginia, when the EPA, who strongly opposed to what is referred to as "mountain top removal" mining, simply set up criteria for water run-off from these mines that would stop the mining without having to actually change the law that allowed the mining. The judge chided the EPA saying,

... "How to best strike a balance between, on the one hand, the need to preserve the verdant landscapes and natural resources of Appalachia and, on the other hand, the economic role that coal mining plays in the region is not, however, a question for the Court to decide."

What the judge meant was since the EPA (an agent for the Executive branch) can't unilaterally impose these restrictions and that he as a judge (an agent for the Judicial branch) can't allow them, then only the Legislative Branch is capable of doing so—and it is through this process that environmental laws should be implemented. Environmentalists howl that it is almost impossible to get laws protecting the environment done this way due to the gridlock and general inefficiency in Washington, but that's simply not the case. Good environmental law, such as the Clean Air Act and Clean Water Act are two examples where majorities in Congress were convinced to do the right thing.

Finally, conservatives understand and believe that advancements beget advancements. It took iron mines to create steel. It took steel rails to make the railroads. It took railroads to bring products to market quicker, and once we could do this, whole industries were born—industries that spawned innovation and jobs, but first someone had to dig an iron mine. Think of Chicago and its large modern skyscrapers where thousands of environmentally conscious workers ply their trades. Those buildings didn't start out that way. One hundred years ago, millions of trees where cut down in Michigan to provide the lumber for their predecessor's framework. In Ohio, large mines provided the raw material to make brick for the facades. With brick and wood, Chicago was built on the banks of Lake Michigan. When Mrs. O'Leary's cow kicked the lantern over, and the place was destroyed by fire, the city was rebuilt with steel. That's right, rebuilt. If no one would have cut those trees down, or dug those sand mines, there would be no Chicago today.

Chapter 49

Public Employee Unions

Conservatives have no beef with labor unions. There are millions of conservatives who are pro-union. I happen to come from a family where my grandfather and his brothers were very conservative in their views, and they were also pro-union. If you are a union-hater, I would suggest that you read the history of our country and you will get a clear view on why unions started, and why they were necessary. Conservatives understand that unions have a legal right to exist and are perfectly within their power and authority to challenge management when they feel worker rights are being violated. Conservatives believe that companies also have certain rights under the law just like the unions. When the two sides are in opposition, the conservative believes that the dynamics of the marketplace and/or a judge's decision will resolve the conflict. When the two sides are in agreement, it's a beautiful thing.

However, there is a certain type of union that conservatives oppose. Public sector employee unions.

Public sector unions are relatively new to the scene. When the labor union movement was born in the 1800s with fellows such as Samuel Gompers leading the way, it was inconceivable that public employees would need, nor should have, the right to collectively bargain. Why? Because, as with private enterprise, there is no profit motive that governments have to exploit workers. Governments can't move away if the terms of the union are onerous, and it was seen as a huge conflict of interest.

If public employees were unionized *and* able to vote, why wouldn't they just vote for politicians who would continually raise their pay and benefits?

And that's exactly what has happened. Franklin D. Roosevelt, no enemy of unions by a long shot, was afraid this would happen. In a letter to Luther C. Steward, then president of the National Federation of Federal Employees, on August 16, 1937, he wrote among other things that he understood the public employees' desires for good wages, benefits, safe working conditions and opportunities for advancement are as important to them as it is for union members of private companies. But he also wrote of his concern when he noted that:

> *"All Government employees should realize that the process of collective bargaining, as usually understood, cannot be transplanted into the public service. It has its distinct and insurmountable limitations when applied to public personnel management. The very nature and purposes of Government make it impossible for administrative officials to represent fully or to bind the employer in mutual discussions with Government employee organizations. The employer is the whole people, who speak by means of laws enacted by their representatives in Congress. Accordingly, administrative officials and employees alike are governed and guided, and in many instances restricted, by laws which establish policies, procedures, or rules in personnel matters."*

F.D.R. knew then what we know today. Once public sector unions are established, it's like putting the fox in charge of the hen house. Proof of this is the extraordinary and robust growth rates for wages and benefits for public sector employees over the past 50 years when compared to their counterparts in the private sector.

In the fall of 2008, the dangers of granting these wage and benefit packages to the public sector unions started to be revealed. As the country headed into what is considered one of the greatest recessions since the Great Depression, revenue coming into the coffers of state treasuries began to fall precipitously. As budgets started to get cut to make up for the resulting deficits, a spotlight began to shine on these employment packages, and the attention was not good for the public sector unions. Here in Michigan, it was revealed that over the past several decades, our government leaders had agreed to pension obligations for these public workers—including the teachers union—of over $40 billion. That number is almost as much as the budget for the State of Michigan for an entire year. Think about that. To pay the pensions for our retired workers, the State of Michigan would have to give up 100% of its revenue for one year. The public sector union bosses are crying because they claim they are being unfairly blamed for fiscal mismanagement of the state finances, and in a sense, they're right. However, the politicians should never have agreed to these lucrative payouts in the first place. But that is exactly the point. They shouldn't have, but they did, because there was no downside for them. Give the unions more pay and benefits and they will back you at the polls. Don't do it and they will see that you are thrown out of a job. What kind of "bargaining" is that?

Conservatives believe that public sector workers should have wage and benefit packages commensurate with their brethren in the private sector. The way to do this is through labor boards who are accountable to the elected officials. If a person doesn't think he or she is being treated fairly, he or she should quit their job and enter the private sector where joining a union and fighting for workers' rights is recognized and respected on both sides of the bargaining table.

"Dad, if the government promises its workers more than they take in from taxes, where do they get the extra money?"

"They borrow it son. I hope you do play shortstop for the Tigers, cause you're going to need the money to help pay off this debt."

Chapter 50

The National Labor Relations Board

There comes a time in every person's life when they pause to assess their personal situation, whether it be financial, physical, or perhaps spiritual, and they say, *"How in the world did I ever end up here?"*

Conservatives not only oppose the concept of a government agency advocating on behalf of labor unions, but are astounded that this "agency" is considered an essential function of government at all. Conservatives look at the National Labor Relations Board (NLRB) and ask themselves, *"How in the world did we end up with an arm of the federal government suing private employers who are not breaking the law?"*

If you were to go to Washington and ask the federal government if they would consider setting up an agency that would "go to bat" for employers whose companies have signed labor agreements giving them a right to bring grievances by the boatload against those same unions, they would laugh in your face. When you tell them you would like to have 1,500 federal employees hired to work for this agency, and you would also like a $282 million budget allocation for this agency every year, they would think you were insane.

Conservatives think the idea of the National Labor Relations Board is insane.

Let's back up a bit. In the 1930s, the labor movement in the United States was needed. Due to greed, corruption, and general disregard for the plight of the worker on behalf of business managers, labor unions were necessary to stop this exploitation. Conservatives who value and respect the dignity of all humans acknowledge this dark past in the life of corporate America and make no effort to try to cover it up. We are not proud of how business managers, many of whom probably considered themselves "conservative," felt that it was okay to treat their workers the way they did. The workers, through threats of violence and even death, fought back and it's a good thing for all of us that they did. Over the next 50 years the unions grew stronger and the wages, benefits, and working conditions steadily improved until they were the best in the world. But just because a union was necessary, and just because it was legal, did not justify Franklin D. Roosevelt setting up an agency with broad prosecutorial rights and its own judicial board. That's right; the agency is both prosecutor and judge.

I can hear the howl from labor leaders now. *"The National Labor Relations Board is bipartisan, and the business community can bring complaints to it as well."* On paper that may be true. If I am a business and I think I'm being treated unfairly by the union representing my workers, I certainly have the right to take that to the board and ask to have my case adjudicated. But why? If the union is breaking the law, why don't I just take them to court? Conversely, if they feel they have a complaint with my company, sue me. The right to use the civil courts for these types of disputes is already codified by the board; that is where all appeals are sent. So why don't we dispense with the board and just take our cases directly to the courts? The unions know full well why, because the National Labor Relations Board, by its very nature, is pro-labor. They have a vested interest in representing labor's interest at the expense of business. In the beginning the board offered a whiff of sympathy to the cause of companies by stating that if a business could operate without being interrupted by strikes, then that would be in the company's best interests. Wow, with that kind of logic I think I'll take two unions at my business and I'll really be profitable. Apparently it made sense to FDR, however, as he signed the bill and the federal government got its agency.

The National Labor Relations Board has become a farce, and everyone knows it. Recently, presidents from both sides of the aisle have nominated board members only to have them rejected by Congress. In what has become a charade, the only way to get candidates through to this highly polarized position is to use recess appointments. But this infighting and bickering is all a sideshow to a recent display of anti-business behavior on behalf of the board that demonstrated to the whole country where their sentiments lie. The Boeing Corporation, located in the state of Washington where it has several unionized facilities, decided (for a number of reasons) to open a new facility in South Carolina, which was entirely their prerogative. The federal government, through the National Labor Relations Board, sued Boeing. The reason? Washington is not a right-to-work state, and South Carolina is. It doesn't matter who won the suit, it doesn't matter who lost. It just begs the question, *"How in the world did we end up with an arm of the federal government suing private employers who are not breaking the law?"* The answer is found in the fallacy of the National Labor Relation Board.

> Full disclosure: I'm in the construction business, and I have the right to hire anyone I want to. For this reason, I choose to hire union

carpenters. Why? Because of their productivity, quality of their work, and work ethic, I can make more money with them than I can with non-union carpenters—at least this has been my experience thus far. As a business owner I listen to their concerns and we work together to find solutions to problems. If my firm is successful, they have jobs. If I'm not, they don't have jobs, and they understand that and try to help me be successful. The system works if both sides trust each other. I have never had a complaint lodged against me by the NLRB and I hope I never do.

Chapter 51

The Glass-Steagall Act

Tony LaRussa, the manager of the Saint Louis Cardinals (among other teams) once said, "It's not the consequences of your decisions, it's the consequences of the consequences." In reference to the Glass-Steagall Act, truer words were never spoken.

The 1933 Banking Act did many things. First, it created the Federal Deposit Insurance Corporation, which, as discussed in the next chapter, is a federal intrusion into an area of business more readily suited to the private sector. Second, the 1933 Banking Act contained four provisions that separated commercial banking from investment banking. Instead of a bank being able to offer stocks and bonds, retirement planning, investment advice, and merchant banking services, they were restrained to the more conservative and "boring" business of taking in deposits and making loans. Over the next 30 years, however, bankers started to get "itchy." They saw their cousins in the "sexy" business of equity trading on the floor of the New York Stock Exchange and the American Stock Exchange, and they wanted in on the action. So, little by little, they pushed back against this law. At first, they bought or established "affiliated" companies who did their trading for them. They approached the regulators and asked, *"Please, just this little bit of action? It's a small part of our banking volume, and we are very conservative."* Someone said "okay" and the camel had his nose firmly under the tent. Next, it was financial planning. *"Oh please, Mr. Regulator, since we are already selling stocks and bonds, can't we advise the people who are buying them on how they should plan for their retirement? We'll make sure that they invest wisely and conservatively. We wouldn't want them to get hurt."* Then a bit later, *"Oh, pretty please, Mr. Regulator, we've developed these really cool instruments called mortgage-backed securities. We know that they are difficult to understand and we know that they seem to resemble a Ponzi scheme, but Standard & Poor's has given them a AAA rating so there is absolutely no risk whatsoever of anyone losing any money."*

In the Fall of 2008, the dominos started to fall. Before it ended, the federal government had to inject a total of $68 billion into the banking system just to keep the world markets from seizing up and causing a global depression.

Now, back to Tony LaRussa. The consequence (or result) of restricting commercial banks to the boring business of borrowing and lending was, it never happened. Instead of holding the banks to the letter of the law, regulators repeatedly allowed this law to be watered down and eventually become ineffective. "Little by little," the banks pushed back on these restraints, until the ultimate consequence was something much different than what was originally intended. Banks were allowed to act like "wildcatters," taking huge gambles with depositor's money. By 1999 the Glass-Steagall Act was repealed, but by that time (for all intents and purposes) it was already dead. It was "wild, wild west," baby, and money was being made hand over fist.

Now let's stop for a second and examine what conservatives think of this situation. Surprisingly, conservatives don't blame the banks at all. They don't blame the exotic instruments the banks came up with to offer customers higher returns, and they don't blame the customers for wanting those returns and buying these crazy ideas. They blame the federal government for two really big errors. First, let's go back to 1993. Remember the FDIC? Yup, by establishing the FDIC, the federal government promised the depositors that they didn't have to worry about their money in these banks anymore. They didn't have the responsibility to monitor a bank's business plans, their balance sheets, their loan restrictions or ways of doing business. Nope, Big Brother now did that for them. They just put their money in any ol' bank that had an FDIC sticker on the door and Uncle Sam would make sure they got their cash back. This transfer of responsibility from businesses and individuals to the federal government was a huge reason why no one really cared to do the hard work and keep banks in line. Second, the regulators whose job it was to REGULATE were either incompetent or asleep at the switch. When mortgage-backed securities (MBS) were introduced into the marketplace, Wall Street wanted to sell them for the highest amount possible. So they had them "rated." They went to companies such as Standard and Poor's, Moody's, and Fitch's, and asked them to give these securities ratings (AAA being the best) so that investors would know the risk they are taking when they bought them. Strange, even though these securities consisted of thousands of subprime loans, the agencies gave them all AAA ratings. Why would they do this? Because they were being paid big fees to do so. If one ratings agency wouldn't give the sought-after AAA, then they would take their business elsewhere, to one that would. The agencies were in the business of making money, and therefore gave the highest ratings possible to stay as profitable as possible. My dad used to say, "If one guy lies, and the other guy swears to it, it's still a lie." If a bank or their brokerage division says the MBS are good, and a ratings agency says so too, they might still be bad. And they were.

Conservatives believe that if the Glass-Steagall Act was administrated the way it was intended, none of this would have happened. However, allowing a bank to morph into something closer to a freewheeling, high-risk enterprise, while at the same time telling the American public that "all is well," is wrong.

In conclusion, it's important to understand that conservatives are not against "freewheeling, high risk" enterprises. Conservatives love these types of companies, and believe that when people invest their money in them, they should understand both the rewards and the risks. However, with Glass-Steagall, the government pulled a classic "bait and switch" with the American public: "Invest in these safe banks," they were told, "We've got you covered." Yeah, covered all right. Covered in an $86 billion taxpayer bailout.

Chapter 52

The FDIC

As with many governmental entities, the Federal Deposit Insurance Corporation (FDIC) was started as a temporary government corporation to get us through a short-term crisis in 1933—and eighty years later it's still around.

Conservatives believe that the federal government does not belong in the insurance business, and if depositors want this coverage, they should pay for it themselves.

The FDIC doesn't seem like that big of a deal. Basically, the federal government requires all banks that want to claim they are "FDIC-insured" and put that sticker on the front door, to pay a premium on the insurance to the FDIC themselves, and then keep their balance sheets in good order. The theory is that it doesn't cost the depositor anything, and that it keeps the banks honest. Neither of which is true.

First, the cost. When the FDIC says that the insurance doesn't cost the consumer anything, they are not telling the truth. The cost of the insurance is paid by the bank and so therefore is part of their overall expenses. In order to make money, these same banks have to charge more for their services—hence, the price is passed through to the customer. This may come in the form of increased fees for ATM use and checking, or for higher interest costs for a loan. But in some way the bank is recouping the cost, and the customer (but perhaps not the depositor) is paying for this insurance. Conservatives believe that if the government would step aside, private for-profit insurance companies could provide this coverage more efficiently and less costly by selling it directly to the depositor. This is the business they are in and it just seems logical that if several companies are competing for this business, it will be done cheaper by them than by a bureaucrat from Washington who has a monopoly.

Second, when a depositor places his money in a bank and gets it insured "for free," it takes away his responsibility to do any due diligence or background check that might show whether a bank is stable or not. If the FDIC were not available, depositors would be compelled to seek a bit of additional information on a bank prior to just blindly turning over their funds as they do now, trusting the FDIC. Conservatives believe that if this small level of scrutiny were required, then the financial disaster that we just witnessed in 2008-2009 might have been averted. Here's why. Over the past ten years, millions of depositors were putting their hard-earned savings in their local banks, and turning a blind eye to the banks' lending practices. Why were they doing this? Because they could; their money was insured by the federal government even if the bank went under. Don't you think that someone would have started questioning the subprime lending practices at their local bank if it was their own money that was at risk? Conservatives envision a conversation over the backyard fence that would have gone something like this.

Depositor: "Hi new neighbor. My name's Fred, what's yours?"

Subprime Borrower: "Mike, nice to meet you. My wife, Marsha, and I just moved in. We have always loved this neighborhood but didn't think we could ever afford to live here, me being a greeter at Wal-Mart and all."

Depositor: "You're a greeter at Wal-Mart? Does your wife work there as well?"

Subprime Borrower: "Nope, just me. My wife decided to stay home with our kids."

Depositor: "Really? I don't mean to pry but I guess I didn't think Wal-Mart was paying that much for greeters these days, guess I was wrong huh?"

Subprime Borrower: "No, you're right. We were pretty surprised that we could afford this place ourselves, but when the lender down at First National said we qualified for the loan, we jumped at the chance. Anyway, with the way housing values have gone up over the past ten years, we feel we can sell the place for a $50 thousand dollar profit in about five years. Well, nice meeting you."

Fred has his money on deposit at First National. He knows that Mike's house was on the market for $200 thousand and he knows darn well that no greeter at Wal-Mart can afford to pay back that kind of loan. Fred, concerned, calls the bank and asks them what their lending requirements are. Stunned to hear that they have loosened their loan requirements to the point where a person with virtually no credit whatsoever can borrow enough to buy a small mansion, he decides it's time to find another bank. After a bit of checking he finds another bank with stricter lending requirements where he feels his money will be safer. Talking it over with his wife, they both decide to move their money to the safer bank. Fred doesn't know it at the time, but several other folks in town are noticing the same thing and they start to pull their money out of First National. Down at First National, they just finished a board of directors meeting. The recent withdrawals are a concern, and when the bank board looked into the reason and were told that the withdrawals were due to depositors' concerns with lending to subprime borrowers, the bank decided to reign in this practice and tighten their lending requirements. When this happened, deposits stopped being withdrawn. This scenario was repeated at thousands of banks around the country and in the end there was no housing meltdown. There was no subprime crisis. There was no default of mortgage-backed securities. There was no collapse of Lehman Brothers. There was no drop in the Dow Jones Industrial Average of seven thousand points. All because the federal government required that depositors ask some simple questions and use their brains instead of simply giving money to the banks and trusting the government to watch it for them.

But what if a depositor doesn't have the ability to perform even the simplest due diligence on a bank? Millions of people, who have money to invest, are incapable of studying a bank's financial statements and make a knowledgeable determination if that bank is solvent or not. If the FDIC didn't "insure" that their money would be safe, is there no other investment vehicle available to these poor souls? They are like Will Rogers who said, "*I'm not so interested in the return __on__ my investment as I am the return __of__ my investment.*" Well, if you want an investment option that is 100% safe, then convert your money to cash and simply put it in a safety deposit box. You are guaranteed that you won't lose a penny. The bank can burn down, and your cash will be safe. It can get robbed and your cash will be safe. It can go bankrupt, and your cash will be safe. You will never have to worry about identity theft or unscrupulous brokers. You will never lose a penny. And the government doesn't have to do a thing.

Chapter 53

Banks and "Mark to Market"

You know conservatives are gluttons for punishment when they are willing to defend bankers as it relates to their capricious treatment at the hands of the regulators.

The banking crisis of 2008 was the culmination of a series of failures on the part of the federal government, the credit agencies, Wall Street brokerage houses, and the commercial banks themselves. The carnage was enormous, the losses were colossal, and the lessons learned are many. Dozens of books attacking the perceived cause of the crisis—as well as each author's remedy to prevent future meltdowns—have been written and I'm sure more are in the offing. Conservatives generally agree that there is some truth to the fact that oversight was lax in many instances; however, the truth remains that more laws will not prevent future crises, and that risk is the inherent nature of the marketplace. In the future, large sums of money will be made, and large sums lost. Removing the risk of losing erodes the possibility of rewards. This chapter will not focus on what happened on Wall Street, but what happened on Main Street.

"Mark to market" is a term many bankers and economists use but my guess is that very few people outside of the financial world are familiar with, or really ever deal with it. However, this accounting principle was more damaging than anything else in prolonging the banking crisis and destroying thousands of small businesses, and by way of that, families.

On the surface, "mark to market" seems quite harmless. It requires companies, (and this includes banks) to carry assets on their balance sheets at the market price for that asset, in lieu of the purchase price or even its depreciated cost. The concern is that companies, under certain circumstances, can enhance the value of their assets, and in turn their net worth, by claiming that an item on their balance sheet is worth more than what they could sell it for on the open market. One of the most egregious offenders of "mark to market" was Enron, who for years chose to hold assets on its balance sheet far in excess of what those commodities were worth, and when federal regulators realized what Enron was doing, it was too late. This was not Enron's sole offense, but it was one of the reasons that it became one of the biggest bankruptcies in U.S. History.

What does "mark to market" have to do with the recent banking crisis and its effect on Main Street?

When the real estate market collapsed, a huge spotlight was directed at the balance sheets of American banks. Examiners (more accurately called "auditors") looked for banks trying to prove that they were solvent by holding assets on their books that were recorded at a higher value than what the market would deem them to be. This scrutiny came at the exact time that the president was giving the "greedy" banks a tongue lashing for receiving the bailout money but, in lieu of lending it out to small businesses, they were holding onto it.

The reason they were holding onto it had nothing to do with their greed. Banks wanted to lend the money, but they couldn't. Why? Well, remember what was happening to the real estate market at that time? Yep, it was in a free-fall. Every time an auditor showed up at a bank to examine the health of the assets on the balance sheet, he/she would require another round of write-downs due to the value of the real estate being sold in the area dropping like a rock. For example, suppose a businessperson built an office building in 2007 for $3 million. If they obtained a loan for 80% of this amount, the bank would have loaned them $2.4 million and the bank would be carrying $2.4 million on its balance sheet as the value of the asset. Now suppose, due to the drop in real estate values, a similar office building had just sold in town for $2 million. The auditor would deem the market value of the building on the aforementioned bank's books as $2 million. Since the bank should have at least 20% equity on every loan, the loan had to be "written down" to 80% of $2 million, or $1.8 million. Just like that, the bank lost $600,000. The auditors would report this back to the regulators who would then tell the bank it had to raise its cash reserves to cover the loss and the only way to do this is NOT LEND MONEY!

Guess what happens when banks don't lend money? Many businesses in their town go bankrupt and have to sell their office buildings. When they do, these buildings are put on the market and sold for a fraction of what the loans on them are worth. When this happens the auditors return, see that this aforementioned office building is not worth even the reduced value of $2 million and make the bank take further reductions. This is reported to the regulators and guess what happens? Yep, the bank is required to raise reserves again. How do they do this? The same way they did last time—by NOT LENDING MONEY. All the while the president is brow-beating them to do so.

"Mark to market" is a great principle for commodity products such as oil, corn, small machinery, office equipment, and the like; for something as illiquid as real estate, it is not appropriate. Four years after the crash of Lehman Brothers and the Wall Street bailouts, Main Street is still struggling with this issue. The President and Congress should take the lead and make an exception for real estate when the underlying loan is not in default and the borrower is otherwise solvent. Unless they do banks are going to increasingly shy away from real estate as a class of assets they wish to finance, and this will not be good for our country.

"Mark to market" is applied because of GAAP. This stands for Generally Accepted Accounting Principles. These are not laws in and of themselves. Conservatives understand that just because something is not GAAP-compliant doesn't mean it's not legal, but no bank in the country would dare go against the auditors and regulators and not follow GAAP. If they did they would immediately draw additional scrutiny to their firms, which would probably result in another round of write-downs, and more reserve requirements, and guess how they would raise the reserve requirements? I think you know by now. Conservatives believe in open markets, and so understand that there is an appropriate level of regulation that is necessary. However, when we see something as harmful as "mark to market" being applied to real estate, we have to point it out and ask that our leaders change this practice.

Chapter 54

Corporate Oversight

If ever there was such a thing as a "silver bullet" that, if shot at a problem, would result in the most amount of good done, with the least amount of time and energy expended, it would be a resolve by investors to never put their money into a company whose CEO is also its chairman.

Conservatives have long understood the danger that arises from this situation. Recently, the near collapse of the financial system has only highlighted what happens when the board of directors, led by its chairman, is "asleep at the switch." There are some who are clamoring for new federal rules to make it illegal for this situation to occur, but conservatives know and understand that most problems will not be solved by more rules. For crying out loud, we have enough rules already. What we need in this case is for investors to do the hard work and start demanding that the companies they invest in get the fox out of the hen house.

First, conservatives understand that the job of a CEO is time-consuming and demanding. They also know that many CEOs are compensated by their boards with certain employment packages that contain stock options and buyout clauses; and here is where things can go wrong fast. It is entirely possible that a CEO can make millions of dollars for himself or herself by hitting short-term goals, while at the same time putting the viability of the company in jeopardy and its stockholders' equity at risk of being wiped out. The chairman of the board of directors, on the other hand, is charged with monitoring the overall long-term health of the firm, and therefore owes his or her fiduciary, or agency, relationship squarely to the shareholders. When both of these roles are occupied by the same person, it doesn't take a genius to see that there is plenty of room for trouble.

In a perfect world, a company's board of directors meets on a regular basis, discusses the direction the company is heading, and charges its executive team (led by the CEO) with making any changes that they feel are necessary to grow the company in terms of sales and profitability; at the same time, the board manages risk so the shareholders' interests are protected. It's a fine line, quite frankly. Raising sales and profits almost always requires taking on more, or at least newer, risk. Doing this in a way that does not endanger shareholder interests requires that the board has a deep understanding of how the company is run and what inherent risks it is already taking. In large companies, this type of information is extremely difficult to ascertain, unless the board is very active and engaged in the company's business (something they usually can't do because they probably have "day jobs" and they most likely sit on more than one board). If, in the best of circumstances, it is difficult, imagine what would happen if the person the board was relying on to give it this information conveniently (for him or her) gave the board, only the information that suited their own interests. Perhaps he or she could bury some bad news in an archaic report for a quarter or two while their compensation package was being renegotiated (read, increased). Perhaps he or she could hide some good news for a quarter or two until he or she accumulated more stock options to be exercised down the road when the good news is finally reported. Or, as was the case with so many banks during the financial crisis, the boards were continually lied to about the safety of their investments in assets such as mortgage-backed securities in sub-prime instruments.

When a CEO is also the chairman, the very person whose job it is to keep the board fully engaged (and informed!) might see doing just the opposite as in their favor. This person (CEO/chairman) also has an additional advantage, and that is an outsized opinion as to who any new directors might be. The chairman's job is to recommend, or support others who recommend, new directors. Obviously, they know that as CEO they are going to have to take directions from these new directors so they are very likely (or at least may be tempted to) "pack the board" with directors who will be friendly to them and their leadership. If this is allowed to happen, then board oversight becomes even less rigorous and they become what is referred to as a "rubber stamp," blindly following the CEO/chairman wherever he/she wants to lead them.

Conservatives understand that there will always be some tension between the management of a company (led by a CEO) and its board of directors (led by a chairman), but allowing both of these positions to be filled by the same person strikes us as a conflict of interest too large to accept. We don't want Washington to step in and try to solve this problem with a bunch of rules that corrupt CEOs can circumvent if they really want to. Conservatives believe that if a company has a combined CEO/chairman, then they should be punished in the marketplace by investors who refuse to buy their stock until this issue is addressed.

Chapter 55

Government Policing of Private Industry

Conservatives believe in a limited role for government. There are certain things that a government should do, and other things that it shouldn't. But one thing that is apparent to conservatives is that when the government decides to police something, the average citizen takes that as a sign that his or her personal responsibility to take care of themselves has somehow ended. They may think that way, but it's seldom the case.

Everyone wants and needs some sort of policing to take place in society. We want someone to insure that our food supply is not poisoned or unhealthy. We need the police to prevent the cars on the road from going too fast and causing great danger to other drivers. And finally, we want prosecutors and courts to catch bad guys and keep them from causing any more harm. But unfortunately, in modern times we have allowed the government to police a whole bunch of things that would be better handled by the private sector. When this happens, the consumer gets the worst of both worlds: lousy policing and the high cost of the same.

In this book, there are several references to the Federal Deposit Insurance Corporation (FDIC). This government agency is on the hook for protecting depositors' money, so they (the depositor) don't have to. And how do they protect depositors' money? By policing the banks using federal regulators. Now let's assume for a moment that the FDIC didn't exist. Instead, consumers bought private insurance to protect their deposits. Let's also assume for a moment that there were no bank regulators. Who would watch out for the safety of the deposits? The one who had the most to lose if a bank went broke—the insurance companies. These companies would then be very diligent in only insuring banks whose practices led to a minimum of losses for the insurance companies and, *voila!*, the problem of protecting the depositors' money (as well as the need for strong banks) would be solved without a single taxpayer dollar being spent. That's the beauty of self-policing.

Critics will claim that the government should provide policing in many areas where conservatives don't believe they have any business being. This includes the securities industry. The stock market used to be a place that was recognized for what it actually is: a highly risky place where a person should only invest money that they could afford to lose. After the great crash of the 1930s the average investor wouldn't touch the stock market with a ten-foot pole. It was then that Congress passed the Security and Exchange Act which was meant to provide federal authority over all aspects of the securities industry. This includes the power to register, regulate, and oversee brokerage firms, transfer agents, and clearing agencies. But business was slow—until the 1970s when things really started to change. As the baby boomers started saving for their retirement they wanted higher yields to give them a bigger "nest egg." They turned to the stock market as an alternative to cash, CDs, bonds, or real estate. They turned to the stock market, but not necessarily to stocks *per se*. They bought mutual funds instead. These "baskets" of stocks were thought to be somehow safer than owning shares in individual companies and perhaps there was some truth to that. But what really happened was that they invested in companies but didn't have to perform any due diligence on them. Instead they relied on the mutual fund manager to do this work for them. The fund manager was now charged with not only watching the stocks of a few firms but of hundreds, which made up the basket of companies that his fund had invested in. At first, firms tried to keep up, but in the end, there was this underlying feeling that the SEC was watching over everyone's shoulder to make sure they were "playing by the rules." In 2007 things started to unravel in a big way. Wall Street firms, who had been under the watchful eye of the SEC, had been found to have deluded the American public with the appearance of propriety in a big way: by selling mortgage-backed securities whose underlying loans were made to sub-prime lenders. Companies such as Lehman Brothers declared bankruptcy when only months earlier they appeared to be pillars of financial strength. Bernard Madoff was found guilty of stealing up to $40 billion of investors' money, and firms such as MF Global were declared insolvent and millions of dollars were missing. What happened? Two things: first, the SEC was thought to have been watching out for this type of fraud, and in hindsight they were simply not able to keep tabs on everybody, as they thought they could. Second, they never conveyed this inability to the millions of investors who trusted the SEC to watch out for their best interest.

Now someone could say, *"Think of how much worse it would have been if the SEC was not there at all. More people would have lost a lot more money."* But this is not the case. If the SEC was not policing the Wall Street firms, the message that somehow the federal government is providing this policing would not have been sent either. Because of this, millions of investors who had no business buying stocks or mortgage backed securities, would have been too scared to do so. And the ones who did would have done so knowing that the risks are huge. Conservatives believe that when the government polices something such as the dynamics of a free market system, where risk and reward go hand in hand, they usually do a poor job, and the ultimate cost of this false sense of security is extremely high.

Finally, there are a large number of private or nonprofit companies and agencies that could provide the same services that the government is, without using taxpayer money, and without this unnecessary intrusion into the private economy. The Better Business Bureau, Underwriters Laboratories, Factory Mutual, Good Housekeeping Seal of Approval, Consumer Reports, Angie's List, Life-Lock, are all examples of non-governmental entities who are in business to protect the public from ne're-do- well companies and individuals.

Conservatives believe that if the government would get out of the business of protecting risk-takers from unscrupulous actors, then the private sector would see this as an excellent business opportunity and provide this same service at a fraction of the cost.

Chapter 56

Campaign Finance Law

Conservatives believe that the Supreme Court got it right when it found that certain sections of the law known as "McCain-Feingold," which prohibited the government from restricting certain independent political expenditures by corporations and unions, was unconstitutional. Our only question was...How could it not have?

Read with me, the First Amendment to the Constitution.

> *Congress shall make no law respecting an establishment of religion, or prohibiting the free exercise thereof; or abridging the freedom of speech, or of the press; or the right of the people peaceably to assemble, and to petition the Government for a redress of grievances.*

In Washington, no one will use five words when 500 will suffice. If you ever have the time or inclination, please read the McCain-Feingold Act (more accurately referred to as the Bipartisan Campaign Reform Act of 2002). When you are through, you will get a glimpse of why the average Joe, like you and me, gets so frustrated at the goings-on in our nation's Capital. You will understand as well that Congress can spend thousands of hours in the minutia of deciding who can give what to whom and when they can do it. They spend millions of dollars writing laws that clearly violate our rights as citizens, and then they spend millions more in court, losing, when all the time the language was so clear: *"Congress shall make no law prohibiting free speech."*

I can hear the howls now.

- *"Spending money is not free speech."* That argument was settled 40 years ago when the Supreme Court ruled it was.
- *"Corporations are not people."* No, a corporation is not a person with flesh and blood like you and me, and neither is a union, but they are assemblies of people. Look at the law, it doesn't prohibit people from assembling; and when they assemble, they have the right to free speech.
- *"Big corporations are drowning out 'the little guy' so his voice cannot be heard."* Well, this may be so, but the ruling also allowed unions to spend money on campaigns as well. Don't they represent "the little guy?"
- *"Elections should be publicly financed so that no one has the advantage over anyone else."* Really? You want to restrict everyone's free speech and only be able to hear from the candidates themselves? My guess is that with no competition from outside groups to keep them honest, politicians would be able to lie during their campaigns more than they do now.
- *"Well, we need to restrict this madness somehow. Campaigns have gotten out of control."* Sorry, can't do that. The First Amendment states...Congress shall make no law prohibiting free speech.

Conservatives are pragmatists. We deal with the facts as they are, and not how we wish they were. It's pretty clear that the

216

Constitution allows associations of people to have free speech rights. This will allow corporations and unions to spend their money on issues that they care about. So let's stop looking for ways to limit free speech and start using it to educate the electorate in a way that we feel is best.

Chapter 57

Free Trade

First, a free trade story. My wife and I were married in 1981. Money was tight, but I really wanted to "deck out" our small home for the Christmas season. So I visited our local discount department store and found a 30-foot string of Christmas lights for $30. Shocked by this price, and not willing to part with two hours wages for so few lights, I decided we would use some other type of decoration instead.

Fast forward to 2011; with our kids raised and out of the house, my wife and I decided that it would be great to have them all come back for Christmas. I remembered my experience of 30 years ago, but thought to myself, "This time it will be different, I've got a lot more money now than I had back then. I'm going to get some of those lights." Off I went to the same discount store, and what a shock I received. Those same lights now came in 100-foot lengths, and the cost? Just five dollars. What made this possible? Free trade.

Conservatives believe that free trade between <u>all</u> countries is a good thing. Unfortunately, trade is often used as a non-military weapon to force our opponents into changing their ways or altering their position on dozens of different subjects that have nothing to do with trade.

One example of this is Cuba. We don't like their government and we want their people to overthrow it. So in 1960 we implemented a trade embargo on imported Cuban goods. Our hope was that it would cripple their economy so much that their leaders would step down, be overthrown, or simply change their position regarding their embrace of communism. Fifty years later, we know one thing for sure: it destroyed their economy. But it also deprived U.S. citizens of the opportunity to enjoy Cuban rum, cigars, sugar, baseball players, and beaches. In the end, the Cuban government did not change one iota. Conservatives believe the only thing that happens when free trade is curtailed is that both sides in the argument lose.

It may come as a shock to some people that many politicians on both sides of the ideological aisle advocate for using barriers to trade with other countries all the time. But politicians who call themselves conservative and approve of sanctioning free trade are acting out of political necessity, not economic reality.

A second example of restraining free trade is called a tariff. Basically a tariff is a punitive tax placed on incoming goods from certain countries, seeking once again to punish such countries for a perceived wrong. For instance, when we feel that China is somehow manipulating the cost of their steel (sometimes referred to in the press as "dumping") and selling it to U.S. manufacturers at an unreasonably low price, hence putting our steelworkers out of work; then politicians from steel-producing states scream for retribution. They ask—and sometimes receive—tariffs to be placed on imported Chinese steel so that it costs our manufacturers more and they end up deciding to buy U.S. steel instead. But what really happens is something much different. Instead of changing their ways, the Chinese might decide to place a tariff on incoming U.S. wine as a way to hurt our wine producers. We, in turn, get mad and place another tariff on a different Chinese product and in the end the result is what is called a "trade war." I think you, the reader, can see where this will quickly end up. Both sides get hurt and there are losers everywhere.

Conservatives believe that the marketplace should determine winners and losers. They understand that from time to time there will be anomalies caused by other countries' governments intervening in the marketplace that temporarily tip the market in one direction or another, and someone will get hurt as a result. Conservatives would encourage all businesses to look at what is happening in their industry on a global scale and take steps to limit the damage to their firm when things such as the aforementioned steel "dumping" takes place.

In conclusion, let's go back to the string of Christmas tree lights. What if, back in 1981, Christmas tree light manufacturers in the U.S. would have convinced the government to place tariffs or trade barriers on overseas manufacturers to protect the jobs in their factories? Yes, today we would still be making those lights here, but if they were $30 per 30 feet in 1981, they would probably cost $50 today. My ability to decorate the house with these bulbs would be severely restricted. Instead, I and 300 million other Americans can buy millions of these really cool lights and have lots of money left over for gifts as well. Some of which would be made in the United States. Free trade is a fundamental principle of conservatism, and should be proudly defended by anyone who understands basic economics.

Chapter 58

English-Only in Public Education

Conservatives are pragmatic. We deal with the facts as they are, not as we would like them to be. The fact of the matter is there are millions of Americans whose native language is not English. Located in communities around the U.S. you will find groups of people who could live their entire lives without having to speak English. Recently, however, there began a movement to make English the official language of the United States. The focus of this chapter is how this would affect just one aspect of our lives—public schools.

The "English-only" movement saddens most conservatives, not because we don't love English, and not because we don't think these kids would benefit greatly if they spoke it fluently. It saddens us because some within our ranks, who call themselves conservative, are willing to sacrifice a higher right for a lower one. Specifically, they are demanding that an autonomous and locally elected school board, with local knowledge and predominantly local funding, be mandated on a federal level to do something they may not want to do. Conservatives know that in almost any other area of our lives we would argue for just the opposite.

This issue is controversial to say the least, and sentiments run high on both sides, but conservatives don't have a national dog in this local fight and we need to stay out of it.

As conservatives know, a government solution to most problems will have unintended consequences down the line that will, at some point, make us ask the question, "How in the world did we end up here?" No one ever knows what these consequences will be because they are unintended, but with the English-only issue, I can start to see a few of them arise.

- Local school boards who want to use Spanish, French, Chinese, or Swahili as one of their tools to educate kids under their jurisdiction would be forced to use English only. What happens when someone is forced to do something they don't want to do? They don't do it well. Who suffers? In this case the kids do, which is the exact opposite of what we intended.
- Mandates usually require time (kids will need to learn English before they can learn *in* English) and this time cannot be used to learn something else—say math, science, or history. In the long run, an argument could be made that the student will be better off if they are fluent in English, and this may be so, but in the short run, they will suffer.
- Mandates require money. Conservatives believe that unfunded federal mandates, which is what this would be, are wrong. If we do have to fund it, then we have the seeds of another federal program that will most likely turn into a boondoggle.

Conservatives can strongly encourage local school boards to consider the advantages of using English-only in their schools. Conservatives can pay for studies that will show how this may be the case. Conservatives have the option of homeschooling their kids or sending them to private, parochial, charter schools if they disagree with how their local school boards handle this issue. Conservatives can run for a seat on the local school board and change their local situation. But conservatives cannot demand that the federal government implement a nationwide "English-only" policy without acknowledging that this is exactly the type of intrusion into state and local control they don't like. There are many things that are legitimate concerns of the federal government. Telling local school boards how to properly communicate with their kids is not one of them.

Chapter 59

Printing Money and Inflation

The Federal Reserve has a printing press, and on that press they can print money. They can print as much or as little as they wish; lately they have been printing a lot of it. Inflation, as of this writing, is low; but conservatives believe that the laws of economics are similar to the laws of nature, and just as gravity is not something that you can change, printing too much money will always cause inflation.

Inflation affects everyone, but few people understand it. Everyone knows that the cost of almost everything we buy goes up and down on a regular basis, but generally, gradually, eventually, it almost always goes up. The rate that it goes up is where we get the monthly Consumer Price Index, or CPI. You hear it announced on the news, and it usually sounds something like this: "The Labor Department released its CPI figure today and inflation for the first quarter of the year was up 1.5% on an annual basis." You think, "Oh that's nice," and go back to your work.

Why does the cost of things go up? The short answer is this: When more money is put into the system and the amount of "things" stay the same, the cost of everything must go up to bring the system into balance.

For instance, if all the goods (things) in the world were represented by just one orange and all the money in the world amounted to just $1, then that orange would cost, or have a value of, $1. Suppose that someone printed another dollar. Now there are $2 in the world but still only one orange. That orange would now cost (be valued at) $2. To carry this illustration out further, what if someone printed $100 and there was still just one orange? The cost (value) of that orange would be $100. You see, the price of goods (things) is determined by the amount of money in the world. The amount is called the money supply by economists.

Why are we printing more and more money if it just causes the cost (value) of things to rise? We have to print more money for two reasons.

First, as economies expand and more oranges are made, printing additional money keeps those oranges from going down in value (the opposite of what just happened when we added dollars and not oranges). This is a very prudent thing to do and governments around the world work hard to keep dollars and oranges in balance.

Second, and this is the one that causes inflation, when a government borrows money, it accumulates debt. The United States government has accumulated $16 trillion in debt and in 2012 had to pay $500 billion in interest to the people who loaned them the money. They didn't have an extra $500 billion lying around to make the interest payment, but they either had to pay it or default on the loan. Since they didn't want to do that, they started up the printing press and simply printed the $500 billion. Guess what just happened? No more things (oranges) were added to the world's supply of goods, but $500 billion just got dumped into the system...and the cost (value) of everything just went up.

This is why it is so dangerous to just keep borrowing and printing money. Eventually you have to print more and more, and the cost of everything simply rises out of sight (inflation). In 2012, the U.S. government spent $1.3 trillion more than it took in. Yep, this money will be borrowed, and in 2013 our interest payment will be $560 billion, not $500 billion. See where this is headed?

Conservatives believe that the Federal Reserve has a duty to act independently of the Treasury and the President to establish long-term policies that will protect U.S. citizens from the ravages of inflation on their savings. Conservatives also believe that the Federal Reserve has been far too concerned in the past with keeping the economy going strong in the short term and pushing the damaging effects of their printing addiction down the road. It looks like we might be coming to the end of that road.

Chapter 60

Taxpayer funding of the Corporation for Public Broadcasting

I love *Austin City Limits*, *Nova, Masterpiece Theater,* and *Red Green*. And I love *Charlie Rose.* Yes, I love all of these programs, but conservatives believe that these PBS programs, like those on any of the other 500 TV channels, should have to be able to stand on their own, without forcing taxpayers to fund them. The same goes for radio. I listen to *Morning Edition* on my way into work every day, and *All Things Considered* on my way home every night. On Saturday afternoon, I listen to *Live at the Met*, and *Car Talk*. And on Saturday evening, you will find me on my back porch with Garrison Keillor and *A Prairie Home Companion*. I love these programs and support my local station with my contributions. But conservatives believe that these programs should have to compete in the open marketplace with the other 250 Sirius/XM stations, or the dozens of local radio shows.

Why? It's only fair, and in the end, the marketplace is where winners and losers should be chosen. Many people would argue that the type of programming found on PBS and NPR is not available anywhere else, and I would somewhat agree. But if they feel strongly about this, then PBS and NPR should be a strong brand when they pitch themselves to the market. Many people believe that it will be destroyed if advertisers hold the purse strings, but I disagree. There are plenty of advertisers for shows that lean either to the left or the right and they all do fine as they fight for market share.

Another argument is that smaller markets (who already have fewer local options for arts, news, and education in the first place and arguably need these services most) are at risk of limiting their programming—or worse, closing their doors. The result would be a loss of this type of information available to those communities. This is simply not true. With Sirius/XM and cable programs, there are dozens of options for the viewer/listener to choose from in almost every genre.

Finally, some folks think that it is necessary to have taxpayers fund PBS and NPR so that folks can get this news and information for free and without commercial interruptions. Really? It's the government's role to provide this? Conservatives don't think so.

The world is changing and so must the Corporation for Public Broadcasting. If any other media outlet approached Washington with their hand out, they would be laughed out of town. If PBS and NPR didn't exist and a bunch of people wanted to start them with government funding, the result would be the same. No, the Corporation for Public Broadcasting enjoys taxpayer funding because, like almost every other government program, once it starts it never ends. There must be something in the water of the Potomac, and politicians must drink it as soon as they arrive in town, because if killing the subsidy for a program that competes with hundreds of other viable private alternatives is hard for them to do, how can we ever agree that anything else should be cut?

Chapter 61

Rich Guys

It seems to conservatives that there is a group of people in this country who are getting blamed for just about everything that goes wrong. It also seems that defending them is akin to defending a murderer or thief. "One percenters," they have been called by some; "fat cats" by others. In the everyday reporting that holds itself up as "news," these people are dealt with, as a whole, like social pariah, stealing from the poor and ruining the whole country in the process. Who are these people? Rich guys.

Conservatives believe that liberals do not understand businesses or the people who own them, whom they are constantly labeling with pejoratives and threatening retaliation for their reprehensible actions. Need evidence? Liberal policymakers are continually coming up with ways to hurt business owners, either through excessive regulation or by directly taxing their business profits.

Businesses pay income taxes only if they have income. If they lose money, they don't pay income taxes. Let's ponder that point. If a business pays taxes, then the taxes are part of its cost structure, just like rent, utilities, payroll and insurance. This cost has to be paid by customers when they purchase the business' product or service. Unlike rent, utilities, payroll and insurance, businesses do not get anything of tangible value back when it pays this tax. If businesses did not have to pay the tax, it could lower its price to the customer, and sell more goods! The business would grow. When it grows, it would hire more people! This would result in higher revenue for the government because individual income taxes would grow.

Liberals do not consider that when they tax businesses, they are hurting the most successful and dynamic part of our economy—small businesses. These are owned by individuals (rich guys) who are taking great risks with their time and money to be in business in the first place. When the government taxes their business profits, they have less incentive to work, and their businesses are not nearly as dynamic (think growing and adding jobs) as they should be.

Liberals and their accomplices in the media seem to think that it's somehow morally wrong to be wealthy. They look at rich guys with disdain, not admiration. When this happens, conservatives know that they simply don't understand wealth creation or preservation. Wealth is created when actions and risks are taken. Most wealthy people have worked really hard and have taken some very big risks to get to where they are today. Most of the time these risks do not pay off, and the entrepreneur loses his or her bet. That's right, most of the time business start-ups fail. So when they do succeed, they should not be punished but rewarded; not looked on with disdain, but applauded.

Conservatives understand that creating wealth through commerce is the only way to raise the net worth of all Americans. Liberals think that somehow government spending can do this. It cannot; only commerce can, and it's the rich guys who are willing to take the risks that are inherent in commerce.

So the next time you see that Gulfstream V winging its way overhead, or that Ferrari racing down some beachfront road, just ask yourself...(if you are fortunate enough to have a job)...

"How many poor people have you ever worked for?"

Chapter 62

American Exceptionalism

America's role in the world is not an easy one to describe, but conservatives believe that we are different from other countries, and yes, we are special. Exceptionally special.

Gordon S. Wood, Professor of History Emeritus at Brown University, put it this way: *"Our beliefs in liberty, equality, constitutionalism, and the well-being of ordinary people came out of the Revolutionary Era. So too did our idea that we Americans are a special people with a special destiny to lead the world toward liberty and democracy."*

These ideals and the necessity to lead the world toward liberty and democracy have not always been appreciated by some here at home. But conservatives are not among them. We understand our duty to come to the aid of countries, or people within countries, and help them in their times of struggle. The decision to do this is not an easy one to make. As a political superpower, we are expected by the rest of the world to lead. This leadership comes with risks that our motives will be questioned and our aid will not be appreciated.

However, our belief in American Exceptionalism allows us to act without being stymied by what leaders of other countries think of us. It's unfortunate that some of our more liberal leaders seem to be more sensitive to what the leaders of other countries think of us, than they are proud of our past accomplishments. America is not a bully—unless you are a dictator. America does not go around sticking its nose in other people's business—unless your business is to cause us harm. America is not the policeman of the world—unless you try to commit a crime and cause great harm to innocent people. America is not arrogant—unless you are on the receiving end of one of our lectures about how freedom and liberty for all mankind is important and worth fighting for.

America is special because we have the military and economic might to actually make a difference in the world. Most other countries don't. So what do their leaders do? They criticize us and lecture us to try to diminish our power and authority. They think this makes them "look big" and generally plays well with their citizenry. But in the end, it is our responsibility to lead. And that we must do.

When conservatives see our leaders apologizing for the decisions that we have made in the past, we are saddened and, quite frankly, a little mad. Have we made mistakes as a nation? Yes. Does that mean that we should second-guess our future decisions and go forward only when we have a majority of other countries on our side? No.

So we say to our leaders: lead, and be proud of America. Other leaders would be scared to death if they thought you actually believed their snipping and whining. They want you to lead. They need you to lead. If you don't, the bad guys will see this as a sign of weakness, and our troubles will be even more grave.

Conservatives understand that America is exceptional, and for that we will never apologize.

I'll never apologize, by Craig Wieland

"America needs to repent,
We have become so arrogant.
I humbly wish to say today,
That I'm ashamed of our past ways."

From France to Egypt, then to Asia,
Our liberal leader loved the praises.
"Please forgive our bully ways.
Let's look ahead to better days."

"We've been too quick to start a war.
I think we need to just talk more.
And we must look with admiration
To the group United Nations."

Back at home we watched dismayed
At this contriteness on display.
When he was done, I looked at Dad.
And when Dad spoke he sounded mad.

"Every time the world's in need
They plead with us to take the lead.
Reluctantly, we use our strength
Avoiding it at any length."

"But in the end, a leader leads
And has to do the toughest deeds.
Though nations like China and France,
Around the problems like to dance."

"We are not dancers in their play,
And we don't see in shades of gray.
The world looks to us to lead.
Not offer weak apologies!"

"When Russia built that Berlin Wall
It was US that make it fall.
When Germans captured ol' Paris
It was US that set them free."

"Taiwan might also want to say
A few words how we don't betray
Or turn and run the other way
When China's might is on display."

"And while we're at it please take note
How Iraq squeezed on Kuwait's throat.
Our critics claimed we wanted oil.
Then why'd we leave Kuwait the spoils?"

"We never colonize or cheat
When we our enemies defeat.
We've never stolen land or claims
Like England, Russia, France or Spain."

"And who's the first to Israel's side
When Iran threatens genocide?
We are standing in the gap
To keep them living on the map."

"And don't forget we built Japan
And Europe with the Marshall Plan.
We could have squashed them like a bug,
But that's not us, we are not thugs."

"Eastern Europe would still be
Under evil tyranny.
'Gorbachov, tear down this wall'
Our leader's words you might recall."

"America has given all
To righteous causes, great and small.
No other nation can compare.
Perhaps our leader's unaware"

"You tell this man that we don't mind
If foreign leaders cry and whine.
We are not sorry for our past.
We'll fight again if we are asked."

"So next time terror threats appear
And foreign leaders quake in fear
Once again they will be glad
That we just act on their behalf."

"Liberal leader so dismayed
That God has blessed the U.S.A.
We don't have to stoop or bow
So get that through your head right now."

More information regarding conservative thinking can be found at :

www.craigwieland.com

If you are interested in having Craig speak to a group or would like to contact him regarding this book, please do so at...

cw@craigwieland.com